THEN
WAS ONE

The U.S.S. *Enterprise* and the
First Year of War

by

Eugene Burns

Harcourt, Brace and Company   New York

A WARTIME BOOK

*This complete edition is produced in full
compliance with the government's regulations for conserving paper and other
essential materials.*

To
JOHN CROMMELIN
and
HIS BREED OF MEN

ACKNOWLEDGMENTS

Others made this book possible. When I left home at fourteen, others helped me to get my education. At school, others taught me to write. When war came, The Associated Press gave me one of the greatest assignments of the war. Aboard the *Enterprise*, such men as Lieutenant Hubert Harden, USN, Commander Richard W. Ruble, USN, Captain O. B. Hardison, USN, and Rear Admiral Thomas C. Kinkaid, USN, helped me gather material and gave me expert counsel. During the writing, Lieutenant Robert Giroux, USNR, helped me shape this book for Harcourt, Brace's hands. Commander Waldo Drake, USNR, of the Public Relations Office, Pearl Harbor, and the Fleet Chief Censor, Lieutenant Commander Murray Ward, USNR, read the manuscript carefully and put up with my unbridled enthusiasms with comparative good humor. The Bureau of Public Relations of the Navy Department provided photographs, many of them previously unpublished, with which to document the story of the *Enterprise*. My wife, Olga, spent many hours reading and rereading the manuscript at its various stages. Finally, I make acknowledgment to the real heroes of this book who helped bring the "Big E" (and my battle notes) out of battle—the officers and men of the U.S.S. *Enterprise*.

EUGENE BURNS

Tantalus,
Honolulu, Oahu

AUTHOR'S NOTE

Of the many fine ships in our Navy doing heroic yeoman service for their country on the oceans of the world, fate allows only a few to become great. Many become famous because they find themselves at the right place at the right time, and they have what it takes. But only a few find themselves at the right place at the right time again and again, until their story is legendary. Such a ship is the *Enterprise*.

To the Navy the "Big E" has been a legend for a long time. To the public parts of the legend are known, but the whole story has never been told. In this book I have attempted to tell that story. It will become obvious that it differs from all other carrier stories in several important respects. First, it is the only carrier story which encompasses the entire first year of the war in the Pacific. The "Big E" was the only carrier there on December 7, 1941—steaming into Pearl Harbor on return from a mission at Wake; and, almost a year later, she was that "one patched-up carrier" in action that Admiral Kinkaid refers to, the only major carrier we had left in combat to hold the long, thin Pacific line. Second, only the *Enterprise* was in every carrier action save one (Coral Sea) in the first year of war. That is to say, no other carrier was at all these places at these times: the Marshalls in February, 1942, Wake later that month, Marcus in March, the Tokyo raid in April, the Battle of Midway in June, the first landing at Guadalcanal on August 7-8, the Battle of the Stewart Islands on August 24, the Battle of Santa Cruz, October 26, and the decisive Battle of the Solomons on November 14-15. Finally, the *Enterprise* story is unique in this respect: it is the only carrier story in book form which is unfinished. The same old "Big E" is still in there pitching and the second half of her story, which cannot now be disclosed for reasons of security, may, when the war against Japan is won, be found to equal the first half in heroism and accomplishment.

There are two small points I wish to mention here. The ranks and rates of most of the officers and men mentioned in the text are outdated but I have retained them because, first, I believe they want it that way and, second, it is an impossible task to keep abreast of the many promotions and advancements effected since the events in this book took place. The other point is the subject of the ship's nicknames. There are only two correct ones, the "Big E" and the "Lucky E," and the former is more often used. I have never heard anyone aboard refer to her as the "Old Lady"; neither has any of the ship's company that I've spoken to. This soubriquet originated in Washington and continues to appear in articles, editorials and news stories; though certain sections of the press and Navy Department may feel that it's a good nickname, the men of the *Enterprise* will have none of it. There was also, of course, "The Galloping Ghost of the Oahu Coast," which made good copy but which no sailor would be likely to use as a familiar name for his ship any more than he would a phrase like "Queen of the Flattops." So when it comes to nicknames for the *Enterprise*, you can take your choice. It's the "Lucky E" or the "Big E" and nothing else will do.

It had been my desire to include in this volume a complete roster of the officers and enlisted men who served on the *Enterprise* in the first year of the war. Such a list would have included nearly six thousand names, and would have required some sixty extra pages as well as many days spent in the compilation of the list by the Navy Department. On neither ground did it seem justifiable in time of war. But when I speak of the exploits of an individual or a group, the men of the *Enterprise* will, I hope, know that I am thinking of everyone from Sky Control to boiler room who helped to make those exploits possible.

CONTENTS

THEN THERE WAS ONE

1

NOVEMBER 28–DECEMBER 31, 1941

1. *Battle Order Number One*

The plane bearing Peace Envoy Saburo Kurusu to the United States was approaching Wake Island. Kurusu could not see the three tiny islets below—Peale, Wilkes, and Wake —strung together in the shape of a wishbone; the curtains in the Pan American Clipper had been intentionally drawn and fastened. Had they been open, he might have seen the new installations of the air base and the uncompleted landing-strip under furious construction. Perhaps he smiled at the thought that the antiquated, pre-World War I guns, which he knew were there, could not be elevated to shoot at planes.

The Clipper settled to a smooth landing and taxied through the lagoon to Peale, from whose newly completed mooring Kurusu was quickly driven in a closed car to the Pan American Hotel. There he signed his name in the register, in English and Japanese, taking a whole page. The Clipper was delayed on the following day due to "engine trouble"; Kurusu cooled his heels in his room. When he finally left to continue on his Mission of Peace to Washington, it was doubted that he had seen the new airfield. If he did manage to see it, he must have noted the absence of combat planes.

At Pearl Harbor, meanwhile, the U.S.S. *Enterprise* was hoisting aboard twelve fighter planes destined for Wake.

3

These she was to deliver, with Marine fliers under the command of Major Paul A. Putnam, to the new airfield. Vice Admiral William F. Halsey, Jr., was in charge of the task force carrying out the mission. The *Enterprise* was his flagship, with Air Group Six aboard.

Like everyone else, the men of the Big E were following the Kurusu mission with interest. Whether or not they believed it to be sincere, they hoped it would be successful. In the meantime they were ready for war—more ready, you will see, than their fellow-citizens have been led to understand.

Visiting the carrier while the hoisting was in progress, I noted that all the battleship linoleum had been ripped off the decks. Layer upon layer of paint was being laboriously scraped off bulkheads and equipment. The color of the ship's hull had been changed from a light to a dull dark battle gray. Inflammables, including most of the ship's comforts, had been removed, save for a piano to which the officers clung. Portholes had been welded shut and the ship made light-proof for blacking out each night while at sea. A more expert seaman would have noted other changes: a de-Gaussing cable to prevent destruction by neutralizing magnetic mines, and parallel lines of communications throughout the ship. Learning its lesson from the British carrier *Illustrious*, the *Enterprise* had replaced cast fittings, which break easily during an attack, with forged malleable metal fittings.

For the past six months, under the able command of Captain George D. Murray, the ship's company had been trained intensively in simulating actual battle conditions, involving casualties from explosions, torpedoes, and bombs. As a result, their ship stood ready. At that time it was the sole striking power of the Hawaiian Fleet detachment.

On the morning of November 28, the *Enterprise* slipped

past Battleship Row and out of narrow Pearl Harbor channel. Significantly, there were no battleships with her that bright morning as she departed for Wake. It was a speedy task force, capable of 30 knots; Admiral Halsey had experimented for months with a hard-hitting air force in which only swift ships accompanied his carrier.

Air Group Six, which had taken off from airfields adjoining Pearl Harbor, made its rendezvous with the carrier when she was well outside the channel. Soon the Big E hoisted the routine fleet signal for aircraft operations and the ship started its turn into the wind to recover its planes.

Air Group Commander Howard L. Young, leading the formation of seventy-odd planes in his Dauntless scout bomber, broke off and dived towards the landing circle. The other squadrons followed suit as their "skippers"—Lieutenant Commanders Clarence Wade McClusky, Jr., of Fighting Squadron Six, Hallsted L. Hopping of Scouting Squadron Six, William Right Hollingsworth of Bombing Squadron Six, and Lieutenant Eugene E. Lindsey of Torpedo Squadron Six—gave the signal.

On a little platform off the stern stood the man who, according to carrier practice, was to "fly the planes aboard." The job of the Landing Signal Officer, as he is called, is an important one and dangerous—as the emergency net beneath his platform attests. He holds in each hand a gridded wire paddle, somewhat larger than a ping-pong paddle, strung with brightly colored strips of cloth—his signal flags.

The ritual of landing aboard a carrier never ceases to fascinate me, though I have seen thousands of landings at all hours of the day and night and under all weather conditions. At its best a carrier landing is a virtuoso performance of perfect co-ordination, quick thinking, and split-second timing. Its demands are one of the reasons why carrier duty is considered tops in naval aviation. Once a visiting Army aviator, one of the best in the Aleutians, stood beside me with his mouth open as he watched his first carrier landings. "I see it, but I don't believe it!" he said. "How can a plane possibly land in that space at that speed without spinning in?"

I once saw a battle-crippled plane make a landing so good—the approach so confident, the turn so beautiful, the position in the "groove" (the imaginary extension of the flight deck) so right—that the crew burst into shouts of praise and handclapping at its completion. In such a landing the pilot gets an "R" or "Roger," meaning "O.K.," from the Signal Officer all the way in—a goal every carrier pilot aims at. I've seen other routine landings so ragged and awkward, with the same mistakes occurring despite repeated wave-offs, that some sailor inevitably mutters: "If they don't *shoot* him down, he'll never get down!"

As for night landings, I've seen them on nights so black that you could not tell where the carrier ended and the water began. They are, of course, the most difficult landings of all and not many pilots had made them prior to the war. The *Enterprise* Air Group pioneered in night carrier landings; today they are a required part of a carrier pilot's qualifications.

The officer on the signal platform of the *Enterprise* this November morning was Lieutenant (j.g.) Hubert B. Harden. He landed the planes with only a few wave-offs, and with no untoward incident. As each plane hit the deck and its hook caught the arresting gear, members of the flight deck crew ran out to direct them towards the bow of the ship.

They are a picturesque lot, these plane-handling sailors. Viewed from the island structure aloft, they appear against the battle-gray deck as swift-moving colored dots in their many-hued jerseys and helmets—yellow for plane directors, green for arresting-gear crew, red for armament and fueling, blue for plane pushers, white for fire-fighters, and brown for plane captains. It's a sight to cause a glitter in the eyes of a Technicolor cameraman.

By the time the last plane had landed and was taxied to its parking spot, the pilots had all reported below to their squadron ready rooms. These are combination waiting rooms, rest rooms, lecture rooms, reading rooms, card rooms, and flight information centers where the aviators spend most of their non-flying time at sea until the magic words "Pilots, man your planes!" send them scrambling topside.

As each pilot doffed his fight clothes and sat down, he was handed a mimeographed sheet. Silence filled the rooms as the import of the message took root. What the pilots read was, considering the date, one of the most amazing documents of the war. Here, printed for the first time, is what they saw:

U.S.S. *ENTERPRISE*

At Sea,
November 28, 1941

BATTLE ORDER NUMBER ONE

1. The ENTERPRISE is now operating under war conditions.

2. At any time, day or night, we must be ready for instant action.

3. Hostile submarines may be encountered.

4. The importance of every officer and man being specially alert and vigilant while on watch at his battle station must be fully realized by all hands.

5. The failure of one man to carry out his assigned task promptly, particularly the lookouts, those manning the batteries, and all those on watch on deck might result in great loss of life and even the loss of the ship.

6. The Captain is confident all hands will prove equal to any emergency that may develop.

7. It is part of the tradition of our Navy that, when put to the test, all hands keep cool, keep their heads, and FIGHT.

8. Steady nerves and stout hearts are needed now.

G. D. MURRAY,
Captain, U. S. Navy,
Commanding.

Approved: November 28, 1941.
W. F. HALSEY,
Vice Admiral, U. S. Navy,
Commander Aircraft, Battle Force.

The Big E's mechanics, already overworked with repair work on their own ship's planes, turned to on the twelve old Marine fighter planes to put them into tip-top fighting condition for Wake Island, which lacked machine shops. Motors were taken apart and reassembled, and ordnance men worked over each plane's four .50-caliber machine guns, for they all required boring, sighting, and adjusting. That done, they wiped their oily hands and took the guns topside to test-fire them. All this meant that the crews had to work day and night, but they were used to that. They knew their responsibility: these Marine planes were the first units in the way of establishing the first island advance aviation base in the Pacific.

Overhauled, the planes were painted dark blue topside so as to blend with the ocean if seen from above, and a light gray on belly and underside of wings, to merge with the sky if seen from below. The small U. S. Navy insignia were brushed out and big white stars in red circles painted on fuselage and wings (our insignia have been changed twice subsequently).

In the ready rooms, conferences and war lectures were held with squadron leaders and Marine aviators. At the same time, a far-reaching anti-submarine patrol was conducted and long search flights were stretched.

Halsey's first battle order was followed by a second, more urgent. It told aviators to bomb, torpedo, and strafe any strange vessel which might possibly endanger the task force. The ship was keeping the 5-inch guns and the anti-aircraft batteries manned twenty-four hours a day. Ammunition was placed in all ready boxes, close by the guns.

This was a tremendous operation. The ammunition was loose and it had to be belted and clipped for all the guns on the ship and for the planes. Men worked day and night to execute the order. Crews broke out bombs and torpedo gangs attached war heads—the business end of the torpedo. Bombs were loaded on dive bombers and ammunition was placed in the fighter planes and in the fixed and free guns of the scout bombers. In addition, each scout bomber had a 500-pound bomb fixed to its belly. This was Halsey's reply to Kurusu and Nomura, talking peace with our Department of State.

Some follow-the-line officers speculated upon Halsey's order. According to Navy Bureau instructions, it was contrary to regulations to land planes on a carrier with bombs— but as for attacking and destroying any ship which might endanger the task force, they favored that.

Thus prepared for instant battle, the *Enterprise* steamed into the west—a course towards Japan she was to embark upon repeatedly in the months that followed.

At dawn, December 2, the ship was 174 miles north of Wake. Major Putnam's fighter planes were poised on the flight deck, ready to take off. All hands who could went topside to watch their departure. One by one the fighters sped down the deck and off the bow, rising into the air. They were followed by Scouting Six planes which were to escort them.

In the early morning light the men on board watched them as they joined up and flew off in formation towards Wake.

Near the island, the escorts waved farewell. A storm was in the making and the scouts returned at once to the carrier.

Afterwards, during the first weeks of war when everything was so heartbreakingly inadequate, the men thought bitterly of those twelve planes out there at Wake. Well, they weren't much, but they were something. They were twelve more planes than the Japs expected, twelve where Kurusu saw none. When the invasion of Wake started, those twelve Marine fliers caught the Japs by surprise, flying their planes into everything the enemy sent from the Marshalls. They flew them until only two poorly patched planes remained against overwhelming odds. The last two planes never came back.

2. *"Please Don't Shoot!"*

The wind rose and the storm hit the *Enterprise* as she started her 2,000-mile journey back to Pearl Harbor where she was scheduled to arrive on Saturday, December 6. The usually calm Pacific behaved like a churning bathtub. When the vessel crossed the International Date Line the weather turned even worse. Then the leading destroyer broke a seam.

The task force was forced to slow down—something which Bull Halsey never likes to do (speed was later to save the *Enterprise* from many a Jap torpedo). However, Halsey is equally famed for keeping plenty of fuel in his tanks. So during the return, when the weather moderated, the accompanying destroyers were refueled and the Big E's return to Pearl Harbor was definitely postponed until midday, December 7.

The ship's company, working sixteen hours a day, moaned because they would not make Saturday night in port. Spending the week-end with the folks at Honolulu, taking a date to the Waikiki Theatre, visiting a River Street honky-tonk, or dancing at the Royal Hawaiian to the swish of palms and the wash of the surf—to have to forfeit such pleasures after nine days at sea was bitter.

At dawn, December 7, the Big E was 150 miles from Pearl Harbor. A scouting flight was launched to fly ahead and cover the entry of the ship into Pearl. At the completion of this flight the planes were scheduled to land at Ford Island in the harbor. Before they manned their planes, pilots were besieged with last-minute requests from those remaining on board to call up their wives with news of their return.

Air Group Commander Young led the flight. In his rear seat was Lieutenant Commander Nichols of Admiral Halsey's staff; he was riding in to make advance preparations for the Admiral's return. The planes fanned out towards the islands of the Hawaiian chain—Kauai to the northeast, Maui to the southeast, and Oahu (where Pearl Harbor and Honolulu are situated) in the center.

The first intimation that something was wrong was a radio message broadcast by Ensign Manuel Gonzales. "Please don't shoot!" they heard him say. "This is an American plane." Gonzales was never found.

More startling was the next radio contact. It came from Lieutenant Earl Gallaher, second in command of Scouting Six: "Pearl Harbor is under attack by enemy planes! May be Jap planes."

Then Admiral Halsey received a message from fleet headquarters: "PEARL HARBOR IS BEING ATTACKED BY ENEMY PLANES X THIS IS NO DRILL."

The incredulity aboard the *Enterprise* was reflected in every man's mind. Everyone had known it was coming, but now that it had come, it did not seem real. "Are we at war?

It can't be true!" It was inane, but it was all anyone could
think to say besides "Those dirty bastards!"

With characteristic decisiveness, Admiral Halsey ordered
the large battle flag flown from the forepeak. The national
colors took the breeze, the Navy's declaration of war. The
ships in the screen saw the flag and they too hoisted their
battle flags. On orders from the Admiral a search group was
launched to seek out the enemy until contact was made with
him.

Meanwhile, the early morning scouts flying into Pearl
Harbor had been swept into grim war. Those *Enterprise*
pilots who escaped death went out to get Japs.

Ensign Edward T. Deacon, after exhausting his ammunition on enemy planes, attempted to land at Hickam Field
during the second wave attack on Pearl Harbor. Wounded
in the leg, he crash-landed in the water, dragged out his gunner, used his radio cord as a tourniquet for the gunner's mangled arm, then pulled out his life-raft and put his gunner in
the boat. After reaching Hickam Field dock, and assuring
himself that the gunner was given emergency treatment,
Deacon made his way to shattered, burning Ford Island,
found the commanding officer and requested to be assigned
to another plane.

Pilot Earl Gallaher, who had been first to radio the *Enterprise*, played cagey. He saw the Jap planes, recognized them,
and ducked low with his slow plane, hugging the water. He
saw the Japs flying in overhead and watched their northerly
course after they had dispatched their torpedoes. Following
them, he saw that they struck out northwest from Barbers
Point, *west* of Pearl Harbor. That was enough. He immediately made up his mind to land for fuel and then go out, locate, and intercept the Jap carrier for the *Enterprise* attack
force.

Gallaher landed at Ford Island and hurried to get gas, but under conditions existing at the base was slow in getting it. He then took off and proceeded on his individual search.

He flew out 175 miles but found nothing. The Japs had shoved off—abandoning their pilots. A Richfield oil tanker, which had been challenged by the *Enterprise* screen that morning, later told how Jap planes dropped in the water near her, out of gas.

Air Group Commander Young recalled his predicament: "There I was flying into those Japs with a lieutenant commander in the rear seat. He tried to get the machine gun out and he couldn't." They made a crash landing in a cane field, but were uninjured.

Lieutenant Clarence Dickinson, Jr., was attacked by a greatly superior number of Jap aircraft upon approaching Oahu, while a heavy barrage of anti-aircraft fire met him from our shore and ship batteries. His gunner, William Miller, kept the enemy planes under constant fire, even after he had been wounded, until he finally reported: "I'm out of ammunition." Without rear seat opposition, the Japs closed in and Dickinson's controls were shot away. Dickinson continued to fight the ship until it went into a spin at about 1,000 feet, at which time he was forced to bail out. From Ewa, the Marine base some twenty miles away, he hitch-hiked to Ford Island. Like Deacon, he reported to the commanding officer and was assigned to an additional search mission to the north of Oahu. This and his subsequent experiences are recounted in his book, *Flying Guns*.

Still at sea, the Big E launched another search and attack group in the afternoon, the first search group having failed to make a contact. A report, although it may have been a clever false enemy broadcast, had been received that an enemy carrier was southwest of Oahu. Scout planes carrying smoke tanks were launched to accompany the torpedo planes and lay a smoke screen to make their torpedo runs possible. After a long and diligent search of several hours, these planes failed to find any enemy ships. By now the sun had set. Reluctantly, low on fuel, they started back to the ship.

"It was as dark as the inside of a goat's belly when we returned to the carrier," reported Gene Lindsey, commanding officer of Torpedo Six (he later lost his life at Midway). "One of my planes flew right over the ship signaling that he could not find it."

Although many of his pilots had never made a night landing before, Lindsey preferred to risk landing on the Big E than to risk not making an airfield. He requested the ship's permission to land his eighteen torpedo planes.

The ship's flight deck was opened and Bert Harden stood out on the little platform, ready to bring the planes in with illuminated wands instead of flags. It was the first time in American naval history that a torpedo plane was to be brought aboard a carrier after dark with a 2,000-pound torpedo. But the pilots were at their best. Despite the pitch darkness and heavy loads, they hit the groove and not even a tire was blown.

The *Enterprise* fighter planes, much swifter, had become separated from the comparatively slow torpedo and smoke-laying scout planes when darkness settled on the water. In charge of that fighter group was tall, blond Lieutenant Fritz Hebel. He found the carrier by the ship's wake, called the ship, and was ordered to take the fighters to Pearl Harbor, since he had sufficient fuel.

Jimmy Daniels, one of those fighter pilots, tells the story:

"About forty-five minutes later we made our land-fall. It was Oahu, but we saw so many fires burning that we thought it must be Kauai. The fires we took to be the usual cane fields which are always burned before harvesting. Under this misapprehension we went to the next island in the chain and recognized it as Molokai. We simply couldn't get it through our noodle that the world had turned crazy.

"We turned around again, low on gas, and headed for Pearl. When we got over Koko Head, we contacted the Pearl Harbor tower about 9 P.M. and told them who we were. They gave us landing instructions. I came in fast, landing on Ford Island.

"The smell was fierce. Mixed with the after-fire smell of water on burned rags was the odor of burning flesh and burning oil. I tried to get some sleep in the evacuated married officers' quarters which were shot full of holes. Two hundred yards away a Jap pilot, killed that morning, was stretched out on the ground.

"Days later chunks of unburned powder about the size of a man's thumb were being picked up at Ford Island. All of the women and children, fortunately, had been evacuated to a bombproof shelter. A little canned grapefruit was all most of us had to eat that day. Early the next morning, I finally got a call through to Helen, my wife. She was up in Manoa valley and away from Pearl Harbor (about 13 miles). She didn't know what had gone on."

A more unusual feat than Daniels' landing was accomplished by two of the *Enterprise* scout bomber pilots. They tried to land at Kaneohe Naval Air Station, across the mountains on the other side of the island from Pearl Harbor. Following the disastrous morning attack, personnel at the airport had trundled out and carefully spaced cement mixers, trucks, old cars—anything which would prevent the use of the field by the Japs. The two fliers, Ensign Bucky Walters and Ensign Ben Troemel, arrived when the field was dark.

"We saw some obstacles dimly," said Walters, "but we thought the landing mat was being enlarged. We had no idea that they were trying to block the field to repel a Jap invasion attempt.

"I swung my plane a couple of times and swerved to one side and then to the other in the half darkness. When I rode to a stop, I had a damn cement mixer almost in my lap."

Ensign Troemel, landing with his brakes, skidded around through the trucks and tractors and also wound up scratchless.

They were surprised when the commandant of the airport met them belligerently with: "What in hell do you birds think you're doing?" When they were taken out in broad daylight next morning and shown where they had landed, their eyes almost popped out.

"If it had been light when we came in, we couldn't have done it!" said Bucky, marveling at the sight before his eyes.

3. *"It's Up to You Carrier Boys Now"*

While Jimmy Daniels was calling Helen, the *Enterprise* was maneuvering off Kauai. On the morning of December 8 she made a rendezvous with destroyers, some commanded by young ensigns with skeleton crews, which had come out of Pearl Harbor Sunday morning.

That evening, low on fuel, the Big E was finally forced to risk going in to Pearl Harbor. Otherwise, or if Pearl Harbor fell to the Japs, it would have been impossible to reach the states.

Not a light was showing as the *Enterprise* slipped into the dangerous channel at dusk. The entire area was covered with a smoky pall and the harbor was enveloped with a thick black scum.

Those who were not on duty stood silently on the decks of the carrier and looked at the grim spectacle. As the *Enterprise* slid past Hickam Field, hundreds of exhausted soldiers stood dully beside pill-boxes. Some shouted derisively:

"Where in hell were *you?*" Behind them stood the charred, mangled hangars, with broken planes inside, burned out and gutted. Millions of dollars' worth of Flying Fortresses were scattered about the field. This is how it looked to one lieutenant commander aboard the carrier:

"Passing Battleship Row was the saddest sight any seaman has ever seen. The first ship I sighted was the *Nevada*, down by the stern. Although badly crippled she was grounded beautifully so as not to block the narrow channel. Her crews were working hard.

"Battleship Row was lying on its heels. The *California* was down, her decks awash. It looked as though all the battleships on the outboard side [they were moored in pairs] had been sunk, while those inboard were saved because of this outboard ship protection. The *West Virginia* was badly hit. The *Tennessee* was hit, but she was an inboard battleship. Outboard of her was the *Oklahoma*, as I remember it, capsized, and it seemed as though she should pen in the *Tennessee*. The *West Virginia* had the *Maryland* penned in. The new plane-tender *Curtis* was hit and there was a fire aft. The fires from the *Arizona* were still throwing up a red hot glow.

"The Pennsy [the flagship *Pennsylvania*] was in drydock. Two destroyers in the drydock—the *Downes* and the *Cassin*—had exploded and burned.

"This did not complete the horrible scene of devastation which scared us to our marrow. The cruisers *Honolulu* and *Helena* were hit. The *Oglala* was turned over; the *Raleigh* was hit and down by the stern under water.

"The sight of this destruction none of us on the *Enterprise* can ever forget. And then there were the ruins of Ford Island, the charred and burned hangars with holes in the roof.

"Apparently Jap intelligence was good. Remember, the *Enterprise* was a day late. The target ship *Utah*, with turrets removed for target practice, might have looked like the *Enterprise* to swift-traveling pilots. At any rate, within twenty-four hours, Radio Tokyo announced the *Enterprise* sunk."

Soon after the *Enterprise* docked, a tanker moved alongside to give her fuel. A ghostly moon rode over the cirrus overcast and gave a thin light through the drizzly rain. Watches were maintained on all guns as there was sporadic shooting in the harbor. A second Jap submarine was reported within the harbor and depth charges shook the ship. It was necessary to make boat trips from island to mainland and the confusion was such as to have these whale boats fired on several times in the darkness.

Before midnight, a rumor swept the ship that the Japs had landed at Fort Weaver; heavy rifle-shooting in that area gave it credence. Next morning's Honolulu *Advertiser* had a banner headline reporting the rumored activity of saboteurs; the story was false. There was a dispatch to the mainland telling of Jap paratroops landing at Barbers Point; this fortunately proved false as well.

Everyone worked madly that night taking on fuel, getting provisions, and stripping the *Enterprise* of every excess, including the admiral's barge and the piano. Each man worked against the threat of the harbor.

Before the *Enterprise* moved from her moorings, a friend visited Assistant Gunnery Officer Mott. They stood on the quarter-deck in the glow of the burning *Arizona*. Men were frantically cutting into the hull of the *Oklahoma* to relieve forty men still alive and into the hull of the *Utah*, where they cut out one survivor.

"It's up to you carrier boys now," said Mott's friend. "Pearl Harbor must be held, and you're all we've got left in the Pacific!"

4. *Christmas Present*

At sea during the ensuing weeks, the *Enterprise* interposed herself between the shaken fortress of Oahu and the Jap fleet, as the island rebuilt itself. It was dangerous water. Submarine contacts were almost continuous; screening destroyers dropped their depth charges and asked questions later. Whales, along with Jap submarines, took a beating. But patrols could not guess. In one instance a two-man Jap submarine maneuvered amongst a school of whales trying to come near Oahu. He didn't.

During this period, the crew read lots of bad news in the ship's paper. The Japs had sunk the British battleships the *Renown* and the *Prince of Wales* off the coast of Malaya with aircraft. The Japs were sweeping down the Straits Settlement on to Singapore. The Japs were taking Hong Kong. After knocking out the air-force in the Philippines and the naval base of Cavite, the Japs were landing troops in the Philippines.

Most of all the ship's company wanted news about the twelve Marine pilots on Wake. Men who had worked on their planes, loaned them clothes, and given them toothbrushes, wanted to know how their comrades-in-arms were making out. The *Enterprise* had a private and personal stake in Wake.

And when they did get the news of the grand but hopeless fight, still in progress, the sailors griped: "Why don't we go in and help them?"

"Why don't we land our planes there?"

"How can we fight the Jap if we don't go where the Japs are?"

To them their patrols seemed aimless and futile; they were disgusted and discouraged clear through.

"If our admirals would get out of the oppressive gloom and smell of Pearl Harbor, they'd fight."

The situation at Pearl was confused. Admiral Husband E. Kimmel had been replaced by Admiral Pye. Commander in Chief of the Pacific Fleet Chester Nimitz had not yet arrived.

By now, two other carriers had arrived in the Hawaiian area to augment the *Enterprise* task force. That added to the disgust of the sailors: "We've got three carriers roaming around doing nothing but patrolling. Let's get at the Japs."

This aggressive optimism was tempered at night when survivors taken aboard by the Big E would jump in their bunks and scream. Then men soberly remembered that Pearl Harbor must be held and that holding it was a real job.

A chart of the Pacific was pasted on the bulkhead off the flight deck. Each morning the ship's position was recorded. Men watched intently. When the task force moved west they were excited and cheerful, when east toward crippled Pearl, silent and morose.

The Marines at Wake were still fighting. As ships were being loaded with supplies for the garrison, Pearl Harbor sent them a message asking: "What do you need?" And the Marines replied: "Send us some more Japs."

Finally, the ships were ready. The *Enterprise*, at sea, got specific orders to proceed west.

When the word was passed on the loudspeaker, "The *Enterprise* is en route to relieve the garrison at Wake Island," men cheered and jumped about in sheer delight.

For two days no word was received from Wake. Admiral Halsey ordered more speed. Men scanned the map on the bulkhead. It was December 23, and one day's distance from Wake.

"We'll make it tomorrow morning."

"What a Christmas present for the Marines!"

"What a present for Tojo!"

Then came the report: "Wake has fallen."

All ships of the task force were ordered to retire to Midway—now the nearest point to the Japanese mid-Pacific line —and re-enforce that garrison which must now be held at all costs.

Those who spoke to Admiral Halsey say that he debated about turning back, despite the order to withdraw and cover the landing of supplies at Midway. In his impotence, they say, he swore a half hour.

The New Year was about to dawn, but there was no cause for rejoicing. The future looked black indeed.

2

JANUARY 1–MAY 8, 1942

5. *The "Maarsharu" Islands*

The Marshall Islands were discovered in the early sixteenth century by the Spaniard, de Saavedra, but they were named after the British explorer, Captain Marshall, who visited them in 1788. The name stuck, even with the Japanese, who call them by their phonetic equivalent of Marshall—the "Maarsharu Shotto," the latter word meaning "group of islands." When the war began, the Marshalls had been in Japanese hands for twenty-three years.

It was just and proper that the Marshalls, early in 1942, should have been chosen as the target of our first offensive in the Pacific, but the decision, of course, was not due to a sense of justice; it was based on sound military necessity. For one thing, of all the Japanese-held islands the Marshalls were nearest to the Hawaiian chain; just as they had been used as the base for the forces which overwhelmed Wake, so they might be used to launch an occupation force against Pearl Harbor. For another thing, the news in the Southwest Pacific continued to be bad: Bougainville, the largest of the Solomon Islands, fell to the enemy on January 22, and Rabaul, the large harbor in New Britain, fell on January 23; the Japs were driving us with incredible speed from the outer defenses of Australia. If we could strike at them in the Central Pacific

22

they might divert their forces from the southwest; they might also postpone any plans they might have against the southeast—the Fiji and Samoa Islands—against which the Marshalls also provided a jumping-off place.

When the *Enterprise* learned that it was to be the flagship of the first American offensive against Japan, the elation among the officers and crew was tremendous. When they were told that the target was to be the Marshalls, they eagerly dug out charts and atlases to master the geography. As to many Americans during the first year of war, those thousands of little dots about which one knew only that they were scattered in vague patterns across vast expanses of water and also that they were "island paradises," were soon to take on a very great and personal importance. Strange places like Tulagi, Wotje, Marcus, Tarawa, Nauru, Guadalcanal, Midway, and Espiritu Santo were fated to become very familiar to boys from Iowa and Kentucky.

The *Enterprise* attack was to be aimed against four targets: the islet of Wotje, Roi and Kwajalein islets in Kwajalein Atoll, and Taroa in Maloelap Atoll. A cruiser and destroyer force was to soften up some of these by bombardment prior to the air attack. A second carrier, the *Yorktown*, was to launch its air group against Jaluit and Mili in the southern Marshalls and Makin in the northern Gilberts.

Before entering upon this mission the Big E had performed a number of other duties during January, such as giving air protection to convoys bound for southwest Pacific bases to help nail down supply routes to Australia. While on this South Pacific duty, Enlisted Pilot Harold F. Dixon with Bomber Tony Pastula and Gunner Gene Aldrich had failed to return to the *Enterprise* after an afternoon search. Alone on the ocean for thirty-four long days the three men fought hunger, thirst, sharks, and madness until they made landfall on a friendly South Sea island. Their heroic story has been memorably told in *The Raft*.

The *Enterprise* now turned toward the Marshalls. As she steamed into Jap territory hour by hour, deeper than any carrier had yet ventured, pilots were ordered to shoot down all suspicious aircraft.

When one of the pilots encountered a strange flying boat and it gave no response to his signals, he fired a burst across its bow. With still no response, he buried the next into the plane. The reaction was instantaneous. Ports and hatches popped open. A New Zealand flag fluttered out and from each opening men threw up a split finger "V for Victory" symbol.

One evening, several days from the target, an officer flicked the radio on in the wardroom just in time to hear Major Paul A. Putnam speak as a war prisoner on Radio Tokyo, saying he was alive and well. Everyone took it as a good omen. "We're going to whack hell out of the bases which raided Wake," said the sailors. On January 31, the ship was one day's run from its striking point.

That evening, at sunset, 250 miles from Wotje, a lone Japanese patrol plane appeared on the horizon. The ship's company knew that the success of this mission depended upon one thing, surprise. Discovered, the Japs could concentrate all the aircraft in the entire Marshalls upon them.

"Surely, at our speed he couldn't fail to see our long wakes," said Lieutenant Commander Mott. His gunnery department was ready for the snooper at the anti-aircraft batteries.

However, the Big E neither changed course nor slackened speed.

Admiral Halsey accepted the desperate gamble because more than anything else in the world he wanted to slap the Jap. "That Yellow Belly is just thinking about his fish and rice," he said. "Let's go and blast them out of the Marshalls."

He was right. The plane faded from sight. American ships must have been the last thing the Jap flier expected to see.

During the night cruiser and destroyer forces were detached to shell Wotje and Maloelap at dawn.

There was little sleep in the few hours between last minute preparations and the pre-dawn launchings. This was to be the first ride against the Japs.

The moon set before dawn. The ocean was black except for an occasional phosphorescent gleam in the wash against the sides of the ship. Just as the horizon silvered with faint light, Lieutenant Commander Wade McClusky, Jr., the square-built commander of Fighting Six, roared over the flight deck with blue flame pouring from his exhaust stacks. McClusky with his attack group was on his way to Kwajalein, 150 miles distant.

Three other attack groups, all planes heavily laden, roared into the west. They would have to hit the enemy hard, simultaneously at four bases, and knock out their air power or the carrier would never survive.

Five minutes after the last group took off, things happened within sight of the Big E. Fighters dived out of the clouds over Wotje and almost at once a thin stream of smoke rose. Then there were more explosions as bombs from fighters and scout planes hit. Then the Jap AA from Wotje got blacker. With long glasses, one could see our fighters streaking in to strafe. This was followed by the thunder of 8-inch shells from cruisers and the noisy 5-inch shells from destroyers. Intermittently, larger explosions occurred as new gasoline supplies and ammunition dumps exploded while the smoke became more dense as oil storage tanks torched.

Scouting Six Commander Hallsted Hopping's bomb was the first to hit—the first ever to be dropped on Jap territory by carrier-borne aircraft. And Hal gave his life because he wanted that bomb to drop true into the well-equipped Jap airfield at Roi. Heavy AA did not daunt him and he rode along with his bomb to 1,000 feet after which he continued his dive to the ground to strafe the fleeing Japs. Within 100 feet of the ground, Jap fighters got on him and shot him down at about 50 feet. Hal crashed in flames.

"If he had to go," observed one of his officers, "Hal would have liked it that way."

Ensign Willy West, who went in with Hal, pressed his attack too. He got a hot reception upon his second attack. However, he did not hesitate to go to the aid of a fellow scout bomber who was being attacked by an enemy fighter. While leaning forward into his sights, he caught a cannon shell in the shoulder from an enemy plane coming in from below. Despite his wound, Willy maneuvered his plane so that the fighter was driven off by his rear-seatman. Although weak from loss of blood, he made a good landing aboard, taxied out of the landing area and sat in his plane until the flight surgeon arrived. (The wound failed to heal and Willy was transferred to Pearl Harbor where the surgeon grafted new skin to the lacerated area to effect a proper closure. At Willy's explicit instructions, the navy doctors removed skin from his belly and in doing so left ". . . —," V for victory. Willy West was later killed in a routine take-off in the Coral Sea.)

Over Kwajalein, Air Group Commander Howard L. Young reported to the ship that he was leaving many beautiful ripe targets for torpedo planes. Admiral Halsey dispatched the first returning torpedo planes—nine, in charge of capable Lieutenant Commander Lance E. Massey. Among the "beautiful" targets were a converted 20,000-ton *Yawata* class liner, a cruiser, a 10,000-ton tanker, a submarine, flying boats, and a seaplane tender.

Before Massey arrived with his slow-flying torpedo planes, he knew the Japs were set. As expected, the Japs opened up a heavy barrage of AA fire and gunfire—shooting with everything they could command from ship and shore.

Without fighters to divert the fire and harass, it was tough. Massey instructed the pilots to fan out, find their targets and hit them. Now, halfway down the home stretch, he found that he was being crowded by one of his over-zealous wingmen. Massey sang out over the air a call which was to become famous: "Oh, no, you don't. That big bastard's mine!"

The b.b. was of course the converted passenger liner.

Only one of the nine torpedoes failed to explode within its target.

So pleased was Massey with his torpedo drop that he couldn't resist letting off steam by diving on and strafing two four-motored seaplanes near the liner with his slow plane. As he recovered from his withering strafing attack which churned the water white, he pulled up in the face of a terrific barrage of AA fire from five machine-gun nests on a small near-by island. He swept his torpedo plane around and miraculously escaped with only two insignificant hits, one in an empty gas tank and the other in his radio transmitter.

Lieutenant Jim Gray, Jr., led a fighter group in to investigate Taroa and strafe it. What he found was a big surprise—an amazingly well-equipped airdrome with parked twin-engine bombers on the runway.

Jim knew that this airport might be a decided menace to the security of the *Enterprise*. Before going in he radioed the ship to send more planes.

Jim was having so much fun shooting up the field and watching the excited Japs scattering before his splattering bullets that he did not notice that he had become separated from his squadron. Not until five nimble-flying Jap Nakajimas caught him, rapping out a snaredrum ruffle on his fuselage. The bullets were patterned so close that they took out whole sections of his fuselage and shot away one trim-tab.

Gray shot his way out, dropping two Japs. Back at the carrier he found that his homemade armor boiler plate was dented with at least fifteen bullets directly back of his head.

It is not hard to imagine the terrific pressure the body is subjected to in dive-bombing. Consider a man who developed a bad rupture but told no one because he wanted to fly more than anything in the world. Such a man was Bombing Six Commander William Right Hollingsworth.

Coming back from Kwajalein, Holly led his dive bombers to Taroa to follow up Jim Gray's work and neutralize the base. He knew the Japs would be set with fighters and AA batteries so he led his outfit to an extremely high altitude and a down-sun position to make his approach at maximum speed. His judgment was correct; his dive bombers escaped an attack from protective fighters who had taken patrol stations over the airfield.

Following the attack, only six more Jap planes ever got off the field.

When Holly returned from his flight and reported to Admiral Halsey on the bridge, the admiral with fervent profanity thanked him and congratulated him on a successful job, well done. Holly left Bombing Six shortly after the ship returned from the Marshalls.

A third group of eight planes, launched to follow up both Gray's and Holly's Taroa attack, was led by Dick Best. When Best's flight reached attack position, they were swarmed over by half a dozen Nakajima fighters who concentrated on the tail-end of the formation.

One of our planes zigzagged across the rear of the formation, protecting his fellow fliers and taking the full blast of the Jap fighters. Then when his squadron mates got into their dive and away, he went in for his share of destruction.

This pilot was Ensign John J. Doherty.

The Jap fighters chased him all the way down but Doherty planted his bomb spank on parked planes in front of the hangar which was now burning fiercely.

Meanwhile, Lieutenant (j.g.) Rawie was attacked by two Japs. He shot down one and then turned on the second and headed straight for him. He held on his collision course and the Jap was forced to pull out but not without damage. Rawie's prop bit a chunk out of the Jap's tail surface and the Jap went down, out of control. Rawie returned to the carrier with only a dent in his propeller.

Another pilot to receive the intimate attention of several Jap fighters was Lieutenant (j.g.) Ed Kroeger. One of the Japs hit him with an explosive shell and it mangled his foot. His rear-seatman, Achilles A. Georgiou, shot that plane down. Then Georgiou himself was hit with a bullet plowing from wrist to elbow. However, he continued to fire with his good arm until their safety was assured. After he landed his plane, the pilot fainted.

Now these pilots returned to the carrier—all, that is, save Doherty. He decided to make a couple of more passes at the Japs.

Van Buren, who saw what was going on, called: "Doug, you had better leave those Japs and come on home."

To this Doherty replied, "These God-damned Japs will never get me," and ducked into a cloud with three of them on his tail.

But they did get Doherty.

6. *The Big E Takes It: Wotje*

During this entire attack the *Enterprise* steamed within sight of Wotje.

The ship had been at General Quarters, with all men tied to their battle stations, since 4 A.M. It was now noon. Only a few planes remained to be retrieved and the vessel was retiring to the northeast at full speed before the Japs could bring up bombers in large numbers from bases deeper within the Marshalls or westward from the Carolines.

The ship's executive officer, Commander Jeter, debated. Should he let half of his men go below and eat hot food and then get back to their battle-stations? Following Dewey's classic Manila Bay example, in which the admiral reportedly retired for a meal during battle, the "Exec" called off General Quarters.

Lieutenant Commander Mott took a quick lunch and went back to his lookout station at Sky Control "because I had a hunch something was going to happen." It was not long in coming.

"Our returning aircraft reported enemy planes bearing roughly on the starboard beam, above the clouds. I advised Captain Randall, in charge of the Marine detachment, to alert every man behind his gun because action was imminent, to starboard."

While men below were eating, the Japs came. General Quarters was sounded and, in the enlisted men's mess, a wild scramble ensued as plates stacked with beans, meat, and potatoes were overthrown. A colored steward, who had been taking a shower, rushed naked through the melee shouting: "Open up, boys, the Japs is comin'!"

The enemy consisted of five twin-engined bombers. They

glided out of a cloud at 2,000 feet shortening the distance with terrific speed.

Their open V formation continued unwavering despite the tremendous bursts of AA shot up from the screen as well as the Big E. The boys had not yet learned to lead enough—it was the first Jap attack on any of our carriers.

One of our fighter pilots, Frankie Corbin, poked his nose out of a cloud, saw the AA fire and dashed right back again.

As the enemy closed, the AA finally began to bite into him. However, the Japs kept coming and dropped their pattern of bombs, at least fifteen, while the *Enterprise* went into violent evasive action, first hard to right and then hard to left. Fountains of water 150 feet high shot up all over the ocean like so many water spouts. One bomb, striking the water close aboard port quarter, ruptured a gas line and started a fire.

The fifth Jap plane, after it had passed, turned to the left, made an S turn and the pilot came in on the *Enterprise* for a strafing attack or a suicide landing. As the ship turned out from under this Jap, the gunners poured everything they had into him. He was seen to be out of control, perhaps dead, but the plane kept on coming in approximately on the course set.

Just as this plane bore down, Lieutenant Art Kelly of Air Plot (the information center for the air department) stepped outside expecting to see specks high in the sky. Then this Jap plane loomed up "just enormous, over the stern. As it came in, it sheared off the tail of one of our parked planes, left its wing on the Number 2 gun gallery and slid over the side into the water," Kelly said.

"Gas from the halved plane shot high into the air and drenched the bridge, while bits of the disintegrated plane hurled 150 feet into the air and one wheel leaped fully 250 feet.

"Fortunately, Lieutenant Roper of the gunnery department was quick," said Kelly. "He ordered: 'Cease firing!' and the high octane gas was not ignited."

A flying fragment hit George H. Smith, boatswain's mate second class, and mangled his leg. However, George kept firing his .50-caliber gun at the Jap until the plane hit the water. Within two hours he died, the ship's company's first battle casualty.

At the height of the attack, Admiral Halsey himself ducked for cover and was considerably chagrined to see the grinning faces of two signalmen who refused to duck.

After the battle, he summoned them to his cabin. "What do you mean by laughing at me during an attack?" he stormed, jutting out his strong jaw. "God damn it, I won't have it! Understand?"

As the two seamen looked their solid discomfort, Wild Bull added: "That's all right, lads. I want more of your kind on this ship who can laugh at danger. From now on you're chief petty officers. I hope you don't mind the promotion."

Long after the Jap planes had blown out of reach, one 5-inch battery kept thundering away.

"What in the devil are you shooting at?" his immediate superior demanded.

"Me? I'm throwing up a barrage, sir. It makes me feel safer."

Two hours later a pair of enemy bombers were sighted approaching at 12,000 feet for a second attack. Skipper McClusky was pursuing them, unable to overtake them with his slower plane.

He did the next best thing. He saw the *Enterprise* 5-inch gun bursts and radioed: "You're high, 300 feet. Now you're on, you're on. . . . You've got him!"

Even though hit and trailing smoke, the Jap kept boring in and released his bomb. It dropped 125 yards on the starboard quarter, causing no damage to the *Enterprise* or her screen.

McClusky by this time caught up with the smoking plane and shot it into the water.

At sunset, 6:35, the *Enterprise* was steaming at high speed out of the danger area. A full moon rose ten minutes later and within fifteen minutes the last combat patrol plane had landed.

The cruisers returned from their shelling. One of them had run into a hornet's nest at Maloelap. Six fighter planes sent to that base had been badly mauled and they could not destroy all the Japs. As a result, Jap twin-engined bombers and dive bombers worked over the cruiser and got one hit on it after a continuous two-hour attack.

That night and the next day the *Enterprise* company prayed for the best bad weather possible. They got it in big measure. It turned foggy, with extremely low visibility, and a Jap seaplane which tried to shadow the force was evaded.

It was realized that all available enemy submarines would be on the lookout for the Big E, and several sub contacts were made. Then, the day before the task force arrived at Pearl Harbor, pilot Rawie bombed and strafed a submarine which surfaced almost in front of his sights.

Before the *Enterprise* returned to Pearl Harbor, reports of the successful raid had been released. But full details remained to be told of the 73,000 tons of enemy shipping sunk, and thirty-five enemy planes shot down, and the two airfields blasted.

As she steamed into the same harbor which had lain torn and bleeding on December 7 and 8, soldiers stood atop pillboxes and cheered. Crowds were massed on Hospital Point, Ford Island, to see the victory flag flying from the Big E's forepeak. Bandaged arms waved happily.

Boys on the *Nevada*, grimy and greasy, trying to get

their ship under way, yelled their hearts out as the "Lucky E" steamed by, largely. Other ships' crews joined in the wild acclaim.

The *Enterprise* was the first ship in from the first victory over the Japs.

7. Rendezvous with Wake

Wake was a fact which the *Enterprise* could not get off her mind. Reminders kept cropping up, like Major Putnam's broadcast. Not long after the Marshall raid the ship heard, also by way of Radio Tokyo, that John F. Kinney, another one of the Marines they had taken to Wake, was a Japanese prisoner. That evening some of the officers drank a toast to Kinney. They lifted their glasses and said: "Good boy, John." That was all. Sooner or later they would help settle the score.

The chance came sooner than expected, in the last week of February. The over-all Pacific picture was still grim. Having overrun Malaya, the Japs were approaching Singapore and spreading down through Borneo, New Guinea, and the Solomons towards Australia. Another diversion in the northern Pacific, particularly if it were in the direction of Japan's homeland, might distract their war lords from further advances in the southwest. An attack on air power and fortifications at Wake, for example, would also have the added effect of blunting the dagger point aimed at Midway.

On February 24, the Big E kept her rendezvous with Wake. In the early morning hours of that day the ship and its squadrons were once more in enemy waters, only a hundred or so miles from the island, ready to make the first retaliatory blow against the Jap where he was holding American territory. The first flight was scheduled to reach Wake before dawn and strike the airfield at daybreak, while a cruiser and destroyer force plastered the island with shells.

Weather upset the timing. When the humidity is high—as it was this morning—the propellers turning up at take-off power create a cloud of vapor which completely envelopes the plane. In addition, the intense flare of the exhaust stacks reflected against the vapor blinds the pilot. It is difficult enough to make a night take-off under ordinary conditions when everything outside is pitch blackness. Under these conditions the difficulties are doubly hazardous.

However, it was known that the cruisers and destroyers would be there waiting for the bomb explosions to open up their own barrage. The dive bombers were ordered aloft, despite the foul weather.

Only a few had been launched when one of the planes, piloted by Lieutenant (j.g.) Perry Teaff, slipped over to the extreme left edge of the flight deck, the left wheel dropped into the cat-walk and the plane crashed over the side. As he went over, destroyer searchlights combed the water for the pilot and his gunner, Aviation Radioman E. P. Jinks. Teaff was picked up but the destroyer after a long search had to report Jinks as missing. Thus the accident not only cost the *Enterprise* the services of a very skillful pilot and gunner but the task force also risked disclosing its position to the Japs through the use of the searchlights.

The pilots who did get into the air could not see out of their barrel of light and flew about aimlessly, hoping that they would not collide, and failed to effect a rendezvous.

In view of the danger to his fliers, Admiral Halsey suspended launchings for thirty minutes.

The cruisers and destroyers meanwhile had sweated out the minutes waiting for the dive bombers to open the assault. Then, as daylight disclosed their position to the Japanese on Wake, the bombardment began. The ships concentrated their fire on seaplane facilities on Peale Island, including a naval air station under construction, the Pan American Airways hotel where Peace Envoy Kurusu had been an overnight guest and which was now officers' quarters, and the Pan American dock where he landed. Since we did not know whether the American civilian workers had been evacuated by the Japanese, the construction gang's camp was spared.

When the bombers and fighters arrived over Wake, fifty-five minutes late, the bombardment was well under way. Fortunately the Japs had no aircraft on the base and the only planes to take to the air were float-type observation planes.

Led by Howard Young, the group commander, the dive bombers rained destruction over the airfield, the surrounding installations including anti-aircraft gun emplacements, ammunition dumps, blast shelters, magazines, and underground hangars. Torpedo bombers, carrying light and heavy bombs, concentrated their explosives on fuel deposits of gasoline and stores together with coast artillery batteries on the southwest side of the islands.

Intent upon creating a maximum of destruction with his three bombs, young Ensign Delbert W. Halsey, flying a scout bomber, dropped his heavy bomb in the first attack and then circled the island. He carefully selected the best target for his two bombs, meanwhile strafing machine-gun emplacements along the beach with his fixed guns. Halsey was distracted from his methodical mayhem by a four-engined Jap patrol plane which he sighted as it broke through the clouds east of the island. Halsey immediately gave chase but he was not able to overtake it. In this predicament, he sent out over his radio: "This is Halsey. I got a Kawanishi five miles east of the island heading straight east and I can't catch him."

Skipper McClusky, cruising at high altitude with his Grumman Wildcat, heard Halsey's transmission and spiraled down through the broken clouds and came out almost on the tail of the Kawanishi. McClusky's accurate fire put one of the Jap's port engines out immediately and polished off the rear-gunner. Then his wingman, Lieutenant Roger Mehle and Radio Electrician E. H. Boyers, took up where McClusky left off. As the third fighter bore into the Jap, his guns blazing, the Kawanishi exploded in his sights. Pilot Mehle ducked under the flaming wreckage and miraculously avoided the destruction of his own plane. When he came back to the *Enterprise* he carried a part of the Jap plane embedded in the leading edge of his wing. It was a hinge fitting with the date 1938 stamped on it.

After ten minutes of merry hell, the bombers pulled out of the island and proceeded to a rendezvous east of the island where they discovered a 100-foot patrol boat steaming in weird zigzags. The planes dove upon the vessel. As the first few planes cleaned off the topside personnel, others would come up from below to man the craft. The Jap vessel was settling rapidly when out of nowhere came a destroyer bent on investigating the target of this aerial circus. A salvo from their 5-inch guns sank the boat. The irate dive-bombers were angry: they wanted the claim of sinking the only combatant vessel at Wake. Four Japanese prisoners were taken—the first to be captured during offensive action on high seas.

One plane was lost in the Wake raid. Ensign Perry W. Forman made a forced landing near Wake with his gunner, Aviation Machinist's Mate J. E. Winchester. It is assumed that they fell into Jap hands.

8. *Minami Tori Shima*

Marcus Island differs from most Pacific islands in that it is not part of an atoll. It is a single, triangular-shaped island, 5 miles around, situated well off by itself about 700 miles

northwest of Wake. From Marcus to Japan proper it is only
989 miles—not, as Pacific and airplane distances go, far at all.
To the Japanese it is known not as Marcus, but Minami Tori
Shima.

To enter the very back yard of Japan was a dangerous
thing to do, but that is just where Admiral Halsey led the
Enterprise on March 4, barely a week after the attack on
Wake. To make up for being late at Wake, Air Group Six
was early for Marcus.

The planes were launched by moonlight and the pilots
made their run in under cover of darkness. The big question
in everyone's mind was: "Are they going to surprise us, or
are we going to surprise them?" We surprised them; several
of our bombs had already hit before their AA batteries began
firing.

A cloud partially obscured Group Commander Young's
target and, rather than wait for the target to show itself, he
continued his swift descent and dropped both bombs and
swept up into a cloud. Immediately afterwards, an enormous
fire started where his bombs had dropped; apparently he had
fired a tank farm. As a result, Young claimed the luckiest hit
of the day.

Besides Young's fire, other large fires were started. In another flaming area, ammunition and gasoline stores added to
the fireworks with frequent explosions of their own making.

It remained for Lieutenant J. D. Blitch to silence a yap-
ping Jap. When the raid began—even before the AA started—
the Marcus radio announcer started calling Tokyo frantically
for help. His screams stopped abruptly when Blitch's bomb
dropped on the administration building from which the radio
operated.

As the carrier pilots retired, Lieutenant (j.g) Hart "Dale"
Hilton sang out in cheerful tones: "This is Dale. My plane
is afire. I'm going to land east of the island, but I'm all right."

Then to returning planes, Hilton and his rear-seatman, Aviation Radioman J. Leaming, waved a vigorous farewell and gallantly gave the thumbs up signal. Their helpless comrades could do nothing more than drop them survivor kits and provisions.

When last seen, Hilton and his gunner were paddling east toward home and away from Marcus. The nearest friendly soil was over 1,500 miles away.

This single carrier thrust against Marcus was completely successful in achieving its aims. It demonstrated the correctness of Admiral Halsey's doctrine of "Attack!" and it caused considerable concern in Japan as to the effectiveness of their defense. It formed one of the first of the many wrinkles that now furrow Tojo's brow.

9. *Silent Partner*

For the *Enterprise*, having gone as far towards Japan as Marcus, there remained only Tokyo. Well, that was a little too much to expect yet. Later, perhaps. In the meantime only Halsey knew what the next mission would be and he wasn't talking.

After Marcus, the Big E drew aircraft replacements and left Pearl Harbor about April Fool's day heading in a northwesterly direction. North of Midway she took up a patrol station and steamed in circles, God and the admiral alone knew what for. The ship's company, wearing tropical clothing, got goose pimples and shivered as the ship moved into the colder latitudes. Low-lying clouds obscured stars at night and sun by day.

Then one morning a carrier was sighted on the horizon. Big E scouting planes, which swooped over it, were dumbfounded; they had never seen such giant planes on a carrier, planes with twin tails and twin engines. The carrier was the *Hornet*. As cruisers and destroyers of the two task forces deployed into a single screen, *Enterprise* personnel noted the strange brown craft lashed to the *Hornet* deck. There appeared to be sixteen.

Conjecture was terrific. "They're B-25's!"

"You're crazy, sailor. A B-25 could never take off with a load—and if it did it could never land aboard again!"

"They won't have to carry a load, you dope, and they won't have to land. They're re-enforcing some land base," one officer said.

"Out here? Which land base!" was the logical retort.

"I'll bet we're going through the Aleutians and deliver them to a secret Siberian base," was the plausible guess.

The aviators joined in the guessing. "Are they using Army pilots on carriers? If so, our careers are over. Let's join the Marines."

Anyway there were sixteen B-25's on the deck of the *Hornet*, that was plain to the eye.

The *Enterprise's* mission was that of workhorse—to patrol the sky and to fight, if necessary. The *Hornet's*—whatever her mission—was that of a carrier which, except for her guns, was in no position to repel an air attack.

Finally a dispatch from the *Hornet*, read over the public address system, assured everyone that she carried sixteen North American B-25 Army bombers with Army personnel on a special mission. That eliminated part of the guessing but there remained: "What special mission?"

"Where is Bull Halsey taking us?" was on everyone's lips.

The weather continued to be foul—heavy seas, foggy, cold and disagreeable—the difference between the rise and fall of the deck being 150 feet. However, the constant searches and anti-submarine patrols were intensified.

And the combined task force still steamed westward!

Three days after joining up with the *Hornet* on April 17, all of the heavy ships refueled from a tanker and at nightfall rang up high speed and headed still deeper west. A glance at the navigator's chart now showed that unless someone made up his mind to change course, and soon, the *Enterprise* and *Hornet* would steam up Tokyo channel.

All burning questions were settled next morning. Admiral Halsey had the word passed over the loudspeaker system that the task forces were going to have "the great privilege of being the first force to strike Japan!"

Men cheered and cheered. Everyone was jubilant. The admiral broke out a pleased grin.

"Trust Wild Bill to take us to Tokyo!" they said. "And, by God, Bull Halsey will see us out again."

Enterprise search pilots doubled their efforts, if such a thing were possible. Upon them depended the safety of the entire mission. They knew that. There was the responsibility too that the mission would have to be achieved by surprise to make it effective. No submarine or flying boat or patrol vessel must see their task force. Too, it was for them to see that we were not steaming into a neatly baited Jap trap, deep in Jap waters. It was no secret that after Pearl Harbor the Jap fleet was virtually three times as strong as our far-flung Pacific fleet, with plenty of submarines for scouting purposes. This force must return.

There was excitement aboard the *Enterprise* and there was fear. Fear of the unknown. Were the tricky Japs ready and waiting for us? Would we be sighted? If sighted would we get away? If we got away would we be pursued by the Japanese fleet?

The plan called for the task force to close near the eastern coast of Honshu, the main island of Japan proper. Then, while the B-25's were raising hell in surprised Japan, the two carriers would retire at high speed to get out of plane range.

The last day broke, dawn became light, and the Big E and the *Hornet* with the accompanying fast cruisers were well out from Japan. But with the dawn, an alert gunnery officer in sky control, looking directly ahead from his high position, saw low on the water directly in the task force course over ten miles away, a small patrol vessel.

Admiral Halsey swore magnificently, changed course and swore some more. He hoped that the Jap patrol vessel in the early dawn had not sighted our force. Then another patrol boat was sighted and planes out on search located many more, including larger vessels.

These patrol boats—former fishing smacks—were about 100 feet long, all conspicuously rigged with radio antenna.

Certain that they were sighted by the Japs, a screening cruiser was ordered to destroy the patrol vessels. The first was a small one. When the cruiser's 6-inch batteries opened up, the salvo splashed around it. As Navy men say: "You can put a salvo on your target, but only God can give you a hit." But the little thing was game and closed distance with the big carrier. With its tiny pea-shooter it replied, although the shot fell far short, making a bit of a fountain.

The cruiser fired a second salvo. This one straddled the little vessel again and rocked it, but the little fellow kept boring in at the large cruiser, popping off regularly with her little gun as she approached, all of her shots falling far short. The cruiser's third salvo disintegrated the patrol boat. Then with the other patrol vessels the cruiser had less trouble. Those seen were destroyed and four Jap survivors were picked up.

Curiously, despite the fact that by the end of the first year of war the Big E accounted for more Jap tonnage than was sunk by both sides in the battle of Jutland, this was the only surface engagement the *Enterprise* was to witness during her first year of the war.

Despite being sighted by the patrol vessels, the combined carrier task force steamed on to Tokyo, the *Enterprise* leading—each mile saving the pilots a gallon of gasoline.

The Flag debated. Should they send the planes out now that the task force was sighted? The enormous planning, secrecy, worry, might count for nothing. And every minute's high speed steaming toward Tokyo endangered the carrier force.

Colonel Doolittle declared that his pilots would damn well take the chance of making Tokyo and flying on to secret Chinese bases. There was no question of turning back.

Two hours after the Jap patrol vessels had been sighted, the *Hornet* was ordered to launch the sixteen bombers. It was decided that the two carriers could not risk steaming deeper into Jap waters without finding, perhaps, a permanent berthing place on the ocean floor. Planes were rocked to put in a few extra pints of gasoline. Each plane was given five 5-gallon tins of gasoline. However, Jap pre-war medals and decorations tied to some of the bombs were not removed.

Plans were revised hastily. Previously Colonel Doolittle was scheduled to take off two hours before the remaining fifteen planes. Loaded with incendiaries, he was to drop them in the dead of night and provide targets for the on-coming fifteen bombers.

Orders given, the *Hornet* turned into the wind, which was from the northeast from Alaska, and put on top speed. The Big E remained to the south on her starboard quarter, thereby winning the distinction of being the carrier to come nearest Japan during the first year of the war. This is one of the least of the Big E's distinctions, but these things mean much to the men of the fleet.

Practically all hands on the *Enterprise* were on the flight deck with every available binocular and long-glass to witness the launching. After what seemed a century, the first heavy

B-25 swept down the half-deck and into the air and commenced a rapid climb round the carrier. That plane was
Colonel Jimmy Doolittle's. The whole *Enterprise* outfit, topside, cheered like a bunch of college kids at a winning touch-
down on the crucial Thanksgiving Day battle.

Having seen that it could be done, everyone on the Big E
prayed that the remaining fifteen would take to the air
equally expertly and uneventfully. The second plane's take-
off by Captain Travis Hoover, however, was not as unevent-
ful. It climbed off the bow in a power-stalled attitude and
the plane settled dangerously within inches of the water.
Miraculously, however, the pilot steadied the plane and
climbed into a circle over the carrier.

Colonel Doolittle had by this time finished his calculations,
dipped low over the *Hornet*, wobbled his wings and headed
into the land of the Rising Sun. The remainder of the planes
with no untoward incidents swept up the deck, one after the
other, and with a minimum of delay headed for Tokyo.

The planes launched, the combined task force immediately
reversed course and withdrew at high speed.

Now everyone hoped and prayed that the sixteen B-25's
would not be overwhelmed by Japanese fighters until they
had delivered their blow. Apparently the Japs knew they
were coming.

Meanwhile, all sets were tuned to Jap shortwave radio
stations. As the elapsed time was hastily reckoned, men would
say: "Now they should be there." "No, give them another
half-hour. They're flying slow to stretch their gas."

Then one of the Jap radio stations rebroadcast the English
speech of two days before: ". . . all I see is beauty, serenity,
and cherry blossoms." And the commentator continued by
pointing out the impregnability of Japan and the immunity
of her industrial areas to air attacks.

While the announcer was still blabbing, the American bombers went in at low altitude. The rest is history.

10. *Then There Were Six*

American planes were hitting Japan's capital on April 23. To the public following the war in the Pacific it was the only good news in an otherwise black month. On April 9, Bataan Peninsula had fallen; by early May General Stilwell's forces had been driven out of Burma, exposing India to attack. The Japanese were obviously moving forces south through the Carolines to prepare a new offensive; their holds in New Guinea, New Britain, and the Solomon Islands area now threatened all Melanesia and our last foothold in the southwest, Australia itself. Then, on May 8, we felt another blow —the *Lexington* was sunk.

This was black news to the whole fleet, but particularly so to the men of the carrier forces. As the first carrier to be sunk, it brought home very sharply the fact that carriers are among the most vulnerable vessels of the fleet. This was a fact which everyone thoroughly understood, but one from which our fleet had so far not suffered. It was true that the *Langley* had been sunk off Batavia on February 27. She had been our first carrier, CV-1, converted from the collier *Jupiter*, which had been commissioned in 1913. But before the war began she was no longer a carrier and had been converted once more, this time to a seaplane tender; she had seen her best days. The "Lex," on the other hand, was one of the biggest carriers in the fleet and had been commissioned comparatively recently, in 1927.

She was riding to her heroic fate just as the *Enterprise* and *Hornet* were steaming back from Tokyo. Late in April, the *Lexington* made a rendezvous with another carrier force in the southwest Pacific, in preparation for what was to be the Battle of the Coral Sea. (Incidentally, this first big carrier battle was the only carrier action in the first year of war in which the *Enterprise* did not participate.) On May 4, the *Yorktown*, which was with the *Lexington*, launched its air group in a successful blow against Japanese ships in Tulagi Harbor in the Solomons. On May 7, both carrier air groups attacked a Japanese force near Misima, sinking our first Jap carrier, the *Shoho*. On May 8, a duel between American and Japanese carrier forces took place with our side making hits on two additional Japanese carriers.

In this engagement the *Lexington* was hit by torpedoes and bombs from Jap carrier planes late in the morning. She managed to keep underway, however, and was believed safe. It was apparent later in the day that she could not continue and our own destroyers had the tragic job of finishing her off. She went down to her gallant end at dusk that evening.

The news of this disaster spread throughout the *Enterprise* like wildfire. After the initial shock, no one talked about it much. But everyone thought about it. They were glad that most of the "Lex" personnel, many of whom they knew as friends of years' standing, had been rescued. They hoped that if their carrier's turn ever came, they would fare as well.

With the *Lexington* gone, there were six major carriers left: the *Saratoga, Yorktown, Ranger, Hornet, Wasp,* and *Enterprise.*

3

II. *The Meaning of Midway*

The Battle of Midway was an attempt by the Japanese to invade the Hawaiian Islands. As the point of invasion they chose Midway, the northwest tip of the Hawaiian chain. Midway is an atoll comprising Sand Island and Eastern Island; it was on these two points that the Japanese hoped to gain a toe-hold for further penetration along the Hawaiian chain towards Oahu and Pearl Harbor.

Synchronized with their move against Midway was an invasion in the far north against the Aleutians; there they attacked Dutch Harbor, turned back, and under cover of fog, they put forces on Kiska and Attu.

Until Midway, Pearl Harbor had never really been safe from invasion. After Midway, Pearl relinquished its primarily defensive role to become an ever-growing, powerful springboard for offensive thrusts against the enemy. Looking back, now that all the events of the first year of Pacific war have fallen into their proper perspective, we can see that the Battle of Midway was one of the really decisive battles of this war. It was to the mid-Pacific what the Battle of Britain was to western Europe, the Battle of Moscow to eastern Europe and the Battle of El Alamein to North Africa—the turning point, the enemy's farthest reach towards success and the point of his fullest power. These great battles marked the climax of a series of dazzling victories for the enemy; they were the fruits of the initial advantage which he obtained by catching us by surprise and not fully prepared. But they were also the end of the series, the apex from which his fortunes curved downward.

The Battle of Midway lasted from June 3 to June 6. It was a contest of air power alone. No contacts of surface vessels of the opposing sides were made during the entire action. Our air power consisted of (1) planes based on three carriers, the *Enterprise, Yorktown,* and *Hornet;* (2) Marine Air Corps and Army Air Corps planes based at Midway; and (3) Navy planes at Midway. Supporting this air power were all the warships, except battleships, we could muster in the mid-Pacific. (It is interesting to note that the decision was made to keep our battle-wagons in other areas of the far-flung Pacific battlefront.) In addition, all the Army, Marine, and Navy ground forces available were stationed on Sand and Eastern Islands to shoot down attacking Jap planes and repel invading Jap troops.

The Battle of Midway was our first big *combined* operation; Admiral Nimitz, who ran the show, summed it up perfectly: "Despite the necessarily decisive part played by our three carriers, this defeat of the Japanese arms and ambitions was truly a victory of the United States' armed forces and not of the Navy alone."

So much for the home team. As for the opponent's line-up, the air power of the Japanese launched against us came from four carriers and from such land bases as Wake or the Marshalls. Accompanying the carriers was a supporting force of battleships, heavy and light cruisers, and destroyers. The occupation force—transports and their protective screen—completed this powerful, menacing enemy force with which the Imperial Island hoped to bring us to our knees.

When the battle was over we had: (1) utterly destroyed the air power the Japs had sent against us—four carriers and all the planes on them; (2) inflicted very heavy damage on their battleships, cruisers, and destroyers; (3) chased their fleeing occupation force back to Japan; and (4) deprived the Son of Heaven of nearly five thousand subjects.

In achieving this victory we (1) lost one carrier and destroyer; (2) expended not quite one plane for every two Jap planes destroyed; and (3) suffered a small fraction of casualties in comparison with Jap personnel losses. Coldly speaking, it was not a great toll for the tremendous success gained, but as I've heard Admiral Halsey say: "The loss of a single one of our boys is to me a major defeat." Halsey, incidentally, was ill at this time; Rear Admiral Raymond A. Spruance was in charge of our carrier forces.

The victory of Midway was the result of real teamwork. At many points during the battle the *Enterprise* had aboard her decks almost as many *Hornet* and *Yorktown* planes as her own. Many of her planes also roosted at times on the other two carriers—so closely were all the units meshed. It is hard to see how any one unit could be said to have played a bigger part in the battle than the Big E, but her role speaks for itself.

I have sketched in the foregoing background so that the reader may keep in mind the over-all picture—the scope of the battle, its nature and its results. The Battle of Midway is too complicated an engagement to recount in full detail here, even if I had a grasp of all the heterogeneous elements and were free to reveal them. Since this book is mainly the story of one ship, this account is the battle as seen through her eyes.

The turning point of the war in the Pacific

12. *Battle of the Boiler Room*

For the *Enterprise*, the Battle of Midway started in her boiler room. Before Pearl Harbor, the carrier had been due for a complete overhaul. That was now out of the question. Meanwhile, war had imposed the strain of high speed steaming, almost constant maneuvering.

Under the watchful eyes of Chief Engineer Harry B. Southworth, worn parts were replaced and breakdowns were anticipated before they could occur. His crews worked thirteen and a half hours daily with no time off for Sundays—ninety-four hours weekly, month in and out—in temperatures frequently over 110 degrees.

While cruising to the north of Midway after a long run from the South Seas, and anticipating Jap action, Southworth decided that one of his boilers needed rebricking. Having the boiler out during action meant reducing the ship's speed by two very precious knots. Besides this, the ship would not be as maneuverable or as flexible for the segregation of individual machinery. But the job had to be done. The order was given and the crews set to work furiously. Normally it takes seven days to rebrick a boiler.

The *Enterprise* task force made a rendezvous with another force on the afternoon of June 2. They did not know they were on the eve of the Battle of Midway.

Early on June 3 Navy seaplanes, scouting west of Midway, sighted a great Jap fleet of battleships, cruisers, and destroyers escorting at least six large troop transports.

At the same time news came of a Jap attack on Dutch Harbor. It was obvious that a big push was brewing. The ship surmised that the Japs were split into several forces; it wasn't hard to deduce that they must have a carrier force, probably near at hand.

Then came the report that a Jap striking force was steaming toward Midway. As the day advanced, Navy Catalinas and Army bombers went out from Midway to bomb the enemy.

"Where in the hell are their carriers?" asked the *Enterprise* boilermen as they worked feverishly in the bowels of the ship.

"Bet the bastards are sneaking down with the fog."

An area of poor visibility existed to the north of Midway. The Jap carriers, it was thought, were streaking in on that course.

Then at 5:45 A.M. on June 4 a report arrived from a patrol plane: "Many planes heading for Midway." This was it.

The sweating men worked more furiously in the boiler room as the Big E changed course toward the general direction from which it seemed the Jap planes were coming.

The Smoke Watcher on Sky Control, who had a talker-phone connection with the engine room circuit, called down: "The pilots have just been called to man their planes."

Soon the Smoke Watcher reported again: "Midway has been raided by the Japs." To show that he was on the job, he added: "There is a lot of black smoke coming out of our No. 1 stack."

The bong-bong-bong of General Quarters was sounded and the ship was dogged down.

"Now, how in hell are we going to get the old bricks out?" demanded a boilermaker.

"Shove them through the escape hatches," replied Louis Hougardy, chief boilermaker.

"Yeh, brick at a time."

The work went on. The old material was sent up through

escape hatches practically a "brick at a time." Similarly, food was sent down to the men through these hatches.

On Air Plot, report came in from a B-17: "The enemy main body has been sighted."

"God damn it," said Lieutenant Kelly. "That information isn't worth a hoot. What is the main enemy force? Where is it? Where's it heading?"

The B-17 added: "Six major ships in the column."

"Now we know everything," added Kelly.

"Dive bombers are taking off," the Smoke Watcher told the boiler room. "There goes Air Group Commander Mc-Clusky. That's the thirty-fourth dive bomber. Hope they find those Japs."

Air Group Commander McClusky searched the conventional square from a 10,000-foot altitude. Visibility exceeded 40 miles, but he did not make contact with the Jap carriers at the estimated position.

He did not know that a Jap observation plane had located the *Enterprise-Yorktown* task force and that the Jap force had reversed its course, retiring to the northwest.

Calculating that he had overshot the estimated Jap contact position, the Group Commander led his thirty-three planes to the southwest and swept to the northwest for more than an hour, expending precious fuel. He looked at his gasoline gauge again and saw that more than half of the fuel was gone. He also noticed that one of the planes with him was smoking.

The decision had to be made: to continue the search beyond the safe limit of his fuel endurance or to return to the ship, gas, and begin again with more definite information.

He knew the significance of his decision. To return to the *Enterprise* might mean that the Japs would follow him and destroy them before they could hit the Jap. Again, the fate of the thirty-three pilots and gunners was the immediate concern of the Group Commander.

"Suppose that my guess is wrong and I fly them into the ocean for nothing," he reasoned. "But, God, those Japs have got to be in this ocean."

Another group commander from another carrier was debating the same question. He turned back with his planes. Some were able to reach Midway and refuel, others dropped in the water before they reached their carrier. Those that remained were saved to refuel and hit the Jap later.

McClusky looked at his gasoline gauge again. He knew that in another half-hour, in this 20,000-foot altitude, the planes could not make it back.

He looked back. Yes, the pilot with the smoking engine was still with him. "He'll never get back," the leader decided. "If he's willing to gamble, so'm I." His mind was made up. He had made what was later officially termed "the most important decision of the entire action."

As the planes swung to the northwest with their commander, the pilots must have thought of their own safety. And like McClusky they must have seen the smoking engine and thought: "If Tony's willing to risk his neck and not turn back, so'm I."

On the *Enterprise* there was concern. Would their attack group be successful? What are the Japs up to? Will they hit us?

In Air Plot it was almost noon. Sandwiches were served. Bert Harden turned to Kelly: "I'll make you a five dollar bet that McClusky finds them. He'll fly his whole group into the ocean before he gives up. And he'll find them."

In the boiler room men were completing their fight against time. Finally, at noon, as McClusky was still searching for the Jap carriers, the battle of the boiler room was won. Oil was turned into the boiler and at last the ship could once more go full speed ahead.

13. *"I've Found the Jap"*

McClusky looked again. Almost halfway to the far horizon he saw a thin thread of white showing on the deep blue water. Unconsciously he increased his speed. It was five minutes past noon.

Sure enough, it was the enemy. McClusky broke radio silence and notified his carrier: "I've found the Jap." He gave the position and then reported the quarry: two large carriers of the *Kaga* and *Akagi* class (the same perhaps which had wreaked havoc on Pearl Harbor); another smaller carrier in the immediate vicinity; destroyers and, farther out, cruisers.

It was all that a dive bomber could ask for. There were the Jap carriers and, when he put his glasses on them, he saw that the yellow decks were covered with planes.

Had he arrived a few minutes later, that deck would have been cleared. Even now the Japs were frantically trying to take off.

At once, McClusky deployed his dive bombers and prepared to attack. He looked back. The pilot with the smoking engine was gone.

The pilot with the smoking engine was Tony Schneider, a happy-go-lucky chap who never seemed to give a damn for anything and would fall asleep most anywhere. However, that impression changed when one saw him in a plane. He was a smooth flier, as good as they come. As a dive bomber, he was "on."

Tony had not flown more than an hour when his engine began popping. He decided to stick with his squadron and drop his 1,000-pound bomb squarely in the middle of a Jap carrier even if it meant carrying it over there in a parachute.

The smoking engine boosted his fuel consumption rate, almost doubling it. The chances of dropping his bomb were slim while the chances of getting back to his carrier—now that he had come this far—were nil.

With McClusky, Tony saw the carriers at 12:05 P.M. It was the perfect answer to a dive bomber's prayer. Broad expanses of flight deck with a bull's-eye insignia, the Red Rising Sun, smack in the center, for aim.

A glance was all that Tony got out of his determined hours in the air. Within sight of the target his engine consumed the last drop of gas, back-fired, stopped cold.

Tony waved so-long to the remainder of the squadron and glided down to a water landing. Within a half-hour, he saw smoke plumes rising from the damaged Jap carriers and Jap planes returning from Midway with no carrier to rest on. And there were Zeros all over the place.

The next six days he spent in a rubber boat. His first question on being picked up (for fortune smiled on him) was: "How'd the *Enterprise* dive bombers make out?"

As McClusky's thirty-three planes deployed, they noted the peculiar disposition of the Jap ships. The cruisers were from 10 to 12 miles away from their carriers, maintaining practically the same relative position to each other but not conforming to the minor course changes of the carriers. At first sight it looked crazy. Near the carriers, however, were destroyers which maneuvered with them. But most strange, there were no Zeros in the air. Not one fighter to prevent them from getting into their diving position! McClusky had expected the Japs to be pouring in from all angles to break up his bombers' dives at their most vulnerable point, the origin.

And yet, 5 miles below, he seemed to distinguish fighters. Actually the Jap was making a desperate gamble. At Coral

Sea, the Jap learned that U. S. bombs are sometimes fused
for instantaneous explosions which peel back the flight deck
but do not sink the ship. The fatal blows were struck by torpedoes. Hence the Jap's answer was to guard against the tor-
pedo-bearing planes which would have to sweep in close to
the water. The plan fitted into the Jap's way of thinking.
For years he had specialized in torpedo perfection. He knew
how effective it can be.

McClusky was right. Those were Jap Zeros far below.
They were now milling about the water like sharks. They
had tasted blood shooting down forty-five torpedo planes in
less than twenty-five minutes. Worse, few of these lost pilots
had a chance to sock their torpedoes into the hulls of Jap
carriers.

As McClusky looked down now, all those carriers were
steaming at 30 knots and not burning.

The first torpedo planes to arrive that morning were those
of the *Enterprise*, led by Gene Lindsey, the lean-faced, quick-
speaking lieutenant commander who had been leader of Torpedo Squadron Six since before the war started. Gene had
taken part in all the Jap action during the first seven months
of the war.

According to normal carrier procedure dive bombers begin
the attack and, then, with the protection of fighter planes, the
slow torpedo planes come in and polish off the damaged Jap
carriers.

Today, however, the fighter escort, much swifter, out-
stripped the torpedo planes. They arrived over the enemy at
22,000 feet and waited for the slower planes for a half-hour
until their gas ran low. Seeing no enemy fighters, the fighting
squadron commander reported: "No combat patrol" and returned to the *Enterprise*.

After he left, Gene's torpedo squadron arrived.

That day the commander was a sick man. During the embarkation of the squadron off Pearl Harbor some weeks before, he had been severely injured in a plane crash. In landing, his plane went over a gun gallery and dropped into the ocean. He was rescued by the destroyer guard. Transferred to the Big E a few days later, he was put on the sick list.

Before the attack, Gene was in the ready room. He still bore marks of the crash, a gash across his forehead, one side of his face badly discolored, the side on which his ribs were taped was still stiff and he was weak from the loss of blood.

When the traveling order came, Gene slipped into his flying gear. Quickly he rehearsed the details with other squadron commanders and with his torpedo pilots.

Gene led his flight directly to the Jap carriers.

His planes were the first to locate the enemy. As they came in low, cruisers some 12 miles from the carriers opened up with anti-aircraft batteries filling the horizon with dark acrid smoke. As he twisted over the water, the Japs fired their main batteries into the water ahead of him, hoping that the splashing water would rise high enough to hit the plane; if it had, the plane might just as well have hit a stone wall.

After the cruisers had poured their heavy fire into his planes, Jap Zeros, capable of twice the speed of Gene's torpedo planes, zoomed in as his few remaining planes maneuvered to sock their shots dead home. It is quite likely that he was shot down before the attack was completely developed.

Perhaps because of Gene's heroism, the men did everything possible to drive their attack home. As the remaining *Enterprise* planes shoved home their attack, gunfire opened on the opposite side. The *Hornet* torpedo planes were now coming in from the opposite direction.

Testimony of the effectiveness of the Jap guard, they withstood this simultaneous attack. Of the thirty planes, but four escaped.

The attack—begun by the taped, weakened *Enterprise* commander—wrote another heroic chapter in the Navy's history. Not a man flinched, not a man made a futile drop at a distance and returned. Instead each pilot maneuvered for a drop or was shot down.

Looking down upon the streaking Jap carriers, the *Kaga* and *Akagi*, McClusky was cool. He addressed the skipper of Scouting Six: "Earl Gallaher, take the carrier on the port." Then to the Bombing Six skipper: "Dick Best, take the starboard carrier."

He looked about him as the thirty-two planes deployed. Then, as they were in diving position, he said: "Earl, you follow me."

As the planes started downstairs, McClusky saw that the third carrier, smaller only in comparison, was now under attack by a group from the *Yorktown*.

McClusky, like Lindsey, led the attack, diving on the leading Jap carrier.

Not far behind him was young Ensign Stone. The fellow looked a little bit like Peter Rabbit with soft white skin and no beard. Certainly in the choice of a team he would not have been the first man picked. And yet, Stone pressed home his attack with great vigor. He rode it close to the ship and his bomb hit smack in the center of the carrier. Those coming behind him saw the deck peel back like a banana, exposing a great section of hangar below. (Later in the afternoon, Stone was to get another hit on a smaller carrier and then complete the battle with two more hits on large cruisers.)

It was not until after the attack was completed that McClusky saw a fourth carrier about 20 miles off. It was apparently from this "sleeper" that the *Yorktown* was to receive damaging blows.

As Big E carrier planes departed, the two large carriers

were burning fiercely from bow to stern and dead in the water. Then suddenly, a huge ball of solid fire shot out of the middle of the *Kaga* and straight into the sky passing through a layer of fleecy clouds. Fliers above this 1,200-foot layer said that the ball of fire shot beyond another four hundred feet. It may have been a gasoline explosion or from readied bombs on the hangar deck.

Upon his return, Admiral Spruance and Captain Murray asked McClusky to report at the bridge.

"By God, we did it," said McClusky. There were tears in his eyes. Perhaps he thought of the men who would not come back. "We sunk those two Jap carriers, and the *Yorktown* boys got theirs. Another small one is still up, though."

After McClusky had made a detailed report, someone noticed blood on his shoulder. "What's the matter?" the admiral asked.

McClusky was wounded. While in combat with two Zeros —one of which his rear-seatman shot down—a 20-mm. cannon shell exploded behind him and two fragments were imbedded in his left shoulder. He had it dressed, and as a result of this wound he was through flying during the Midway battle.

Later, Admiral Spruance observed: "McClusky is the outstanding hero of the Midway battle. His decision to go on and find the Jap decided the fate of our carrier task force and our forces at Midway and perhaps at Pearl Harbor and the Hawaiian Islands."

14. *Then There Were Five*

By a stroke of luck for the Japs, their fourth carrier was untouched when planes from our carriers hit and fired the three enemy carriers. Planes from this unfound carrier shadowed the *Yorktown* just as our planes, led by McClusky, were attacking the three Jap carriers.

Shortly after noon, word was received at the *Enterprise* bridge: "Twenty enemy planes are coming in." Within two minutes, the *Yorktown*, less than 6 miles away, was seen to open fire. Black bursts filled the air.

There were actually eighteen enemy planes. Eleven were shot down by fighters before their bombs dropped. Seven managed to get through but, even so, one was polished off by a daring fighter who braved the *Yorktown's* AA fire. Anti-aircraft fire destroyed another. A third, presumably while under fire, dropped its bombs into the sea and fell after it in a curving, flaming burst. A thin black streak remained for an instant.

Four Jap bombers aimed their bombs and then got away.

A great column of smoke rose from the carrier and it mushroomed at about 3,000 feet. There was little breeze.

From the Big E three hits were counted. It seemed that the third struck amidship and then there was a big flash out of which a column of smoke rose.

The *Yorktown* pilots who landed aboard the *Enterprise* reported that their ship had received a bomb hit in the stack. An enemy plane, they said, released the bomb after a wing had been shot off. This hit caused a temporary loss of power and the *Yorktown* stopped dead in the water. Much of the smoke came through the stack directly from the damaged firerooms. Although it started a large oil fire, these fires were controlled speedily and she was able to make 19 knots.

Meanwhile, cruisers and destroyers were dispatched from the *Enterprise* force to give added AA support to the *Yorktown*.

At this time Lieutenant Sam Adams, who had left the York on a search late in the morning and discovered the presence of the fourth Jap carrier, returned from the search and landed. He was in the process of refueling and rearming when the second wave of Jap dive bombers approached the ship. With only thirty gallons, he relaunched to defend his ship. As he cleared the ramp and rolled his wheels up, twelve to fifteen torpedo planes escorted by fighters moved in.

Sam shot down one of the attacking planes as it reached its dropping point, close to the water and near to the *Yorktown*.

Again the sky was spotted with black bursts. This time there was almost twice as much and the rumbling and thundering of guns was incessant.

Jap planes came tumbling out of the skies. As each fell, it trailed a plume of red smoke.

Five of the planes got close enough to launch torpedoes but they were shot down before they could return. However, the *Yorktown* was hit again.

Bravely and efficiently she fought her fires and put them out, but the ship took on such a list that she had no power for counter-flooding and it was thought that she might capsize. In order to direct the other ships of the task force, Admiral Fletcher transferred his flag to a cruiser.

The *Yorktown's* tragic end came on the morning of June 7 and she went down gallantly.

The news of this disaster filled the *Enterprise* with gloom. The *Yorktown* was her sister ship, ordered by the Navy the same day as the Big E, out of the same appropriation, according to the same specifications. The Big E mourned the loss of her comrade-in-arms.

15. *The* Yorktown *Avenged*

Up to the time that McClusky's "I've found the Jap!" was heard, the absence of information regarding the position and numbers of the Jap carriers, during the four-hour period from eight that morning to noon, left the American forces completely in the dark. It was assumed that our Midway searches by Catalinas and Flying Fortresses had failed because of interception by Jap fighter planes.

A half-hour before noon, having received no information from our attack group, Rear Admiral Frank J. Fletcher directed the *Yorktown* to launch a search to the west to relocate the Jap carrier force. The search was launched only some thirty minutes before the first attack on the *Yorktown* was made.

To Lieutenant Samuel Adams of the *Yorktown* Air Group, a redhead who had been a light heavyweight wrestler at the Naval Academy, goes the credit for making possible the avenging of his ship's destruction. After hours of flying Adams made the report which gave the exact location of the fourth Jap carrier. This was after 2 P.M.

Besides identifying the vessels—one carrier, one battleship, three heavy cruisers, and four destroyers—he gave their speed, course, and location. The report was complete, concise, accurate—one of the best single jobs of scouting of the war in the Pacific. Low on fuel, he then returned to his ship and landed just in time for the second attack described in the previous chapter.

Because of Adams's report, an *Enterprise* attack group, augmented by remnants of the *Hornet* and the *Yorktown* dive bomber groups and led by Squadron Commanders Dick Best and Earl Gallaher, intercepted the Jap carrier at Adams's estimated position.

Dick Best had become skipper of Bombing Six when Hollingsworth left it after the Marshalls' action in February. He was a big fellow with a temper, but he got over it just as fast as it came. He had plenty of ability and the men in his squadron knew it, so he could tell them what was what and it would stick. One might well say that Dick's sole interest in life was aviation. At the end of the month, when flight-time totals were logged, as squadron commander he was always among the high-time pilots.

This was Dick's second attack of the day. As he had done that morning with McClusky leading, Dick pressed home his attack unswervingly. He did not know it, but this was the fourth and last Jap carrier, to which the Jap planes attacking the *Yorktown* would come home to roost. He went into his dive. It was a hit!

When the air group was through with the carrier, it had been hit repeatedly and left burning fiercely. That was one carrier no Jap planes would land on that day. In addition, a battleship was hit and set afire.

The *Hornet's* attack group arrived a short time later and thought it needless to waste further bombs on the carrier which was already so seriously damaged. It concentrated its attack on the damaged battleship and left a cruiser afire.

Once again, Tony Schneider sitting off on the horizon in his rubber raft was treated to the spectacle of far-away plumes of smoke.

On his return from the mission, Dick Best reported to the Big E flight surgeon saying that he did not feel up to snuff. He had coughed up some blood the previous night and had not been able to sleep. He explained that his chest and lungs caused him considerable discomfort at high altitudes.

The doctor was alarmed. Whenever pilots come to him, it is usually something bad. He gave Best a thorough examination and immediately isolated him in the sick bay. The examination showed that the aggressive skipper had an acute inflammation of the lungs.

The other two doctors agreed that Best was dangerously ill and temporarily out of aviation. Dick refused to admit that it was serious. He was crushed at the prospect of being grounded. Up to the end, including the day of his departure from Pearl Harbor to a mainland sanitarium, he stoutly maintained: "It's nothing that I can't lick. These damn Sawbones can't keep me out of the cockpit."

Dick Best was another member of that early brave band who burned themselves out in service to their country. They either met death after writing records in flame, like Hal Hopping at the Marshalls and Gene Lindsey at Midway, or they wore out their physical frames like Hollingsworth and Best. These men and their comrades must have felt that they were fighting the war by themselves. In a sense, they were. It was a long time before *enough* fresh blood and *enough* new ships appeared on the scene; to them it must have seemed as if these things would never come. Those I knew personally never said so, but I knew they thought so. The great day finally did come of course, but it was none too soon. The enemy meantime had had plenty of time to make the final job all the harder. Honor to Dick Best and his breed for holding the far-flung Pacific front so that we might live.

16. *"Well Done"*

On June 6, Sam Adams was launched with a large group of "visiting" and "local" dive bombers from the *Enterprise* to attack a group of damaged ships reported 300 miles northwest of our carriers. They found a light cruiser. With the Emperor's blessing and damned fine ship handling, the Jap cruiser avoided being hit. Throughout the dive bombing attack it spouted AA fire in considerable quantities.

Only one plane was hit—the pilots did not know which one. When all got back and counted noses, Sam was missing. His shipmates felt his loss keenly. "Too bad," said one, writing an aviator's epitaph, "Sammy would have enjoyed smashing the *Mogami*."

This attack marked the end of the Big E's combat action in the Battle of Midway.

Thinking of Sam and the other brave pilots lost in combat took the edge off the summary of the battle action issued by the captain's office:

Attacks by the *Enterprise*, the *Hornet*, and the *Yorktown* bombers Saturday, June 6, on the enemy completed an air action covering three days.

Enemy losses as a result of our action on Thursday, June 4, are estimated as one carrier on fire and badly damaged; three carriers sunk, one large armored ship or battleship and one heavy cruiser damaged.

Of the carriers sunk, one was the *Akagi*, one was probably the *Kaga*, and one was the *Hirvu* class.

June 6 we picked up two small enemy forces bound for home. The first was two heavy cruisers and two destroyers headed southwest. It was bombed during the forenoon with hits reported.

The second group was two heavy cruisers and three destroyers. Of these, one heavy cruiser of the *Mogami* class was wrecked and abandoned. Other smaller cruisers received bomb hits. One destroyer was sunk and others were strafed by fighter planes.

Our carrier groups have done a wonderful job in spite of heavy losses suffered on Thursday in the initial attack which decided the fate of the battle of Midway. The follow-up blows on our retreating enemy were carried out with great determination. The performance of our ship leaves nothing to be desired. You have again helped to make history.

Well done.

4

JULY 30–SEPTEMBER 30

17. D-Day: Assault

In early July the Big E put in at a South Sea island. There
a terrific swapping fest with the natives ensued. Seamen, who
were not allowed to go ashore, lowered old razor blades,
shorts, tennis shoes, and skivvies to natives in outrigger
canoes. Up on their strings would come *tapa*, beads, coco-
nuts, and in one instance a sailor's uniform. Trading was terrific; within an hour a coconut went for a dollar.

Leaving the island, the *Enterprise* effected a rendezvous
with transports and then steamed west. She remained within
sight of land a full day until the *Wasp* and another carrier
arrived with escorting men-of-war and more transports.
Those on the bridge will never forget seeing the whole horizon suddenly fill with scores of ships.

The destination was Guadalcanal. The day, "D" or "Dog"
day as it was called, was to be August 7. But before any landing could be attempted on Japanese-held soil, a rehearsal was
necessary. This, after all, was the first offensive of the war
against the enemy which involved ground forces of the
United States. Our assault troops had not yet had their bap-
tism of blood.

A large area was marked off at an island base. First, carrier bombers zoomed in, dropping coral-blasting bombs.

Then strafing fighter planes plowed up the sand. Ships lobbed shells into the area. After this, swarms of Marines beached with landing barges. It made no sense to the natives, who watched it all from afar, bug-eyed, particularly as the Marines all shouted and yelled and then departed.

Because of the need for urgency, the landing of supplies and testing of communications was not rehearsed. These two factors were to give trouble later.

As the large flotilla approached the Jap-held Solomons, Lieutenant Commander W. E. Townsend, the Big E's flight deck officer, transferred from the *Enterprise* to the flagship as liaison officer to direct the air traffic, instructing aviators which areas should be softened for Marine landings and later occupation.

On the flagship from which the landing operations were commanded, the whole staff was tense—waiting for the first action. Filtering through every mind were the two thoughts: Are we about to spring a tremendous surprise on the Japs? Or are we steaming into a sudden death trap? It seemed unbelievable that this slow-moving armada would go undetected. The Japs had too many submarines, too many long-range, coal-burning patrol schooners and patrol planes—planes which could fly a day and a night. They had been encountered more than once by our Catalina patrol bombers.

The weather was again typical *Enterprise* weather: it rained. When it did not rain, fog rested over the entire area. *Enterprise* patrol planes had difficulty launching, and it was necessary to keep up a ceaseless patrol.

The tenseness increased as the slow convoy approached Tulagi, known to be a strong Jap base. Surely there would be submarines, perhaps a terrific air battle and maybe a sea battle. Supposing the Japs had some of their new 35,000-ton battleships at Truk, which was not far away . . . ?

Everyone was up long before dawn, August 7, and as

morning drew near the sodden sky cleared, the stars came out, and the day was perfect for flying. The languid beauty of the scene—tropical islands, soft coral-filled sea, high green mountains with purple valleys, the small native settlement on stilts—all seemed incongruous, altogether too peaceful.

Then, on the flagship, alert lookouts reported enemy seaplanes warming up with running lights on—ready for their morning patrol around the many islands. The late take-off and the running lights meant but one thing: the Japs knew nothing of the presence of our armada.

Meanwhile, the *Enterprise* was within spitting distance of southern Guadalcanal. Her dive bombers were loaded and in the air to bomb enemy land positions and strafe beach resistance.

As the Jap props whirred, *Enterprise* planes arrived. The Japs challenged our ships with green and red shore lights. When we failed to give the proper response, a Jap battery opened up. As though a signal switch had been flipped, the bombardment was on.

Heavy naval units began pitching shells into prearranged shore positions while destroyers raced in, firing like mad, and raked the enemy seaplanes before they were air-borne. The weak Jap fire was silenced quickly and what little AA existed was shelled into silence by air and surface force.

Much of the Jap force ashore consisted of Korean laborers —virtual slaves of the Japanese, brought to build the airfield which was within two days of completion—and they dropped their breakfast and scrammed. Their Jap overlords perhaps set the example, for few Japs opposed our Marine landing.

It was a good sandy beach for the landing. By now, two hours after daybreak, the day was full of warm sunshine. The mountains reared even higher into the sky and were a brighter green. Six miles away was forested little Savo Island, a miniature of South Sea beauty.

The Guadalcanal landing proceeded according to plan. That is, the job of getting the helmeted and grenade-carrying Marines ashore was a complete success. But once ashore, each Marine was off to get him a Jap. That left no one to unload the supplies which came in later cargo ships. This was to prove costly for us.

At tiny Gavutu and Tanamboga, the Japs were tipped off by the bombardment of Guadalcanal and resisted. *Enterprise* planes were dispatched to soften up the cave-like positions. In one instance, communications between the pilots and the flagship failed and pilots did not know where the Jap strong-points on Gavutu were.

At times our pilots returned to the carrier with their bombs because they did not know where to drop them, even though enemy targets remained in the heavy jungles. Too, it was difficult for our pilots to differentiate between friendly and enemy troops.

The landings proceeded without major opposition until two in the afternoon, when twenty-two big twin-engined *Nakajima* 97 bombers escorted by *Mitsubishi*-type Zero fighters swept out of the sun at about 12,000 feet elevation.

On the *Enterprise*, one heard Slim Townsend report: "Enemy bombers overhead, maybe twenty." Next: "Pardon me, your announcer is going under the table." Then after a fifteen-second pause: "Townsend speaking. One Jap Nakajima is plunging in flames on the Florida side of our task force. Oh, oh! A second is dropping closer to the *McCawley*. Both are spewing white smoke. No one hurt. No ships damaged. But plenty of our own anti-aircraft fragments are plunking in the water around us thick and fast."

Within two hours, nine Jap dive bombers attacked. Probably because our AA had been so intense on the first attack, these fellows picked an isolated destroyer. It received a 250-

pound bomb hit on her after gun turret, but the ship continued under her own power.

Enterprise fighter planes first intercepted these raiding planes. Typical was the work of Lieutenant (j.g.) Firebaugh's and Radio Electrician Rhodes' six-plane division. They chased the Japs for forty-five minutes towards Buka, northern Bougainville. Finally these *Enterprise* fighters overtook the Jap bombers and their fighter escort. As Firebaugh and Rhodes split for a three-plane attack from either quarter, the quicker Zeros reversed courses, climbed rapidly and jumped Firebaugh's section. Rhodes' three-plane section meanwhile shot down three Jap bombers and smoked three others. Rhodes then was engaged by Zeros and in the general melee the remaining Jap bombers escaped.

Our fighters were outnumbered three to one by these swifter and more maneuverable Zeros. Rhodes' group managed to shoot its way out but Firebaugh and his wingman, Stevenson, were shot down. (The third plane in his section was forced to make a water landing due to fuel exhaustion. The pilots had chased the Japs too far.)

Firebaugh knew that the Japs machine-gunned pilots as they dangled helplessly from their umbrella, and jerked the cord at low altitude. He hit the water hard and injured his back severely. However, he managed to rid himself of the heavy parachute and slowly fought his way ashore through glass-sharp coral.

In the water landing, most of his clothes were torn off by the impact and he was therefore exposed to the blistering sun.

Friendly natives found the black-haired pilot crawling along the beach. They treated him well, but Firebaugh was unhappy. Under his supervision, natives built him a raft and on a cool cloudy morning he set out for the Russell islands, determined to get back to Guadalcanal, island by island, injured back notwithstanding.

As he was on the water, paddling slowly with the current, the sun came out and he was broiled to a crisp. Painfully he made the Russell shore, almost knocked out by the effect of his frightful sunburn. While crawling around in a dazed condition, he was again found by friendly natives.

This time, natives accompanied him and he arrived at Guadalcanal safely in the night. He was transferred to Pearl Harbor and when the *Enterprise* returned to that port, after her damaging August 24 battle, Rhodes found him a month later in a plaster cast, madder than a hornet.

"I want to get out of here and get me a Jap," Firebaugh told Rhodes. "I tell you, I'm all right."

18. *Holding Battle*

Due to the delay in unloading supplies, the transports and cargo ships with their protecting force—the carriers with their screen—were required to stay in the dangerous area longer than was anticipated. The night of August 9, the carriers and their screen retired for a fueling rendezvous, which was very lucky for them indeed.

Four cruisers remained with the transports—the Australian *Canberra* and our ships, the *Quincy*, the *Vincennes*, and the *Astoria.*

It was known that the Japs had a force steaming slowly into the area. When darkness came, the Japs raced in at incredibly high speed.

"The first any of us knew," said Slim Townsend, "was when General Quarters was sounded on the *McCawley* at 2 A.M. Cannonading had begun already toward the entrance of the channel, off Savo, about 6 miles away. They were big

guns and we could follow the course of their red-hot projec-
tiles.

"What the Japs had we did not know.

"We could see shells arching into the ships and then flames
and then vast explosions. The great flashes lit up the entire
sky. A person got sick inside just looking at the destruction.

"It was a rolling hell of gunfire and explosions mixed with
her thunder. I knew men were being blown to bits against
this soft velvet backdrop of a tropical night. It was cool, but
I sweated.

" 'I'll bet we're giving the Japs hell,' a senior officer re-
marked. That made me mad, although I hoped he was right;
we're too damn optimistic.

"It was frightening. I saw a warship get hit badly and a
big mass of fire sprang up from where the shells had hit her.
For us on the helpless transports and for the Marines, everything depended upon the outcome.

"As we saw those flashes gradually go farther away, we
knew that one side had driven off the other to the northwest,
but we didn't know who had won. No one knew whether to
cheer. We dared not.

"No matter who won, many of our men must be dead or
mangled and in the water.

"After the battle it became extremely dark, and began
drizzling slightly.

" 'We must have won, or the Japs would have picked us
off,' an officer observed. That made sense.

"And yet it was not dark—it was only that our eyes were
strained. It was impossible to keep them off one cruiser
which was burning fiercely. Hours later, when dawn came,
there was still that red glow in the sky.

"We were completely in the dark. We didn't know if the
Japs had driven off our screen; if they had, then our large
transport group was nothing but mincemeat for the Japs. If

our carriers were gone, the Japs would come back at their leisure and pick us off.

"There was no one to answer our questions until late the next morning. At 5:30 our transports started picking up boats and lighters, preparing to move out. That tipped us off regarding what had happened that night.

"We first learned that the Australian cruiser *Canberra* was sunk. Then, before the transports pulled out that afternoon, with their holds still partly full of supplies desperately needed at Guadalcanal, it was learned that the *Astoria*, the *Quincy*, and the *Vincennes*, as well as the *Canberra*, were sunk.

"Home seemed a long ways off to a lot of us left at Guadalcanal that night."

Stung with the audacity of the American landing at Guadalcanal just when their large and vital airfield was nearly completed, the Japs tried desperately to wrest back the field. Two days before the Guadalcanal landing, Catalina bomber crews had occupied the Santa Cruz islands. Augmented by B-17 searching parties, they now sought out the enemy's position. Although repeatedly attacked, they carried their work out fearlessly and reported the movement of a considerable Jap force to Guadalcanal. The increased amount of shipping at Rabaul and in the Shortland area north of the Solomons, indicated that something big was brewing. Added to this, the Jap air raids upon Guadalcanal became much heavier.

On August 23, American planes located a force of five large transports with accompanying heavy cruisers, light cruisers, and destroyers. Our accompanying carrier at this time—the *Saratoga*—launched an attack group but due to the distance and the Japs' change of course, the attack group failed to make contact. Their gas was so low they were forced to land on Guadalcanal where they were picked up by the "Sara" at noon the next day—the day of the first sea battle in the holding of the Solomons.

While these planes were returning, the *Enterprise* launched a morning search group from her position east of Guadalcanal. Two Jap submarines were sighted, proceeding at a southerly course at 18 to 20 knots. They crash-dived and escaped. Several Jap seaplanes were spotted by our fighters and shot down. This indicated that the Japs were moving down in a wide-spread fan toward our operating area, that the submarines were advance scouts and that Jap patrol planes were keeping even closer check for their attack groups.

The second *Enterprise* search group in midafternoon produced several major contacts. Lieutenant Commander Charlie Jett, commanding officer of Torpedo Squadron Three, reported a Jap carrier about 250 miles to the northeast. It was the *Ryujo*. He and his wingman at once maneuvered into position and without fighter protection made a horizontal run on the small carrier. Little or no damage was inflicted. Several of the remaining scout sections streaked across the sky to attack the same carrier when they intercepted Jett's report. Coming in by pairs, they were easily driven off by more maneuverable Jap planes which also had more fire power.

The second contact made was with a much larger Jap striking force by Lieutenant Ray Davis. After his contact report, he and his wingman went after the leading Jap carrier. The two bombs dropped with undetermined results either close aboard or in the after part of the ship. There was heavy AA fire and while retiring the two men were jumped by protecting fighters. "The Jap Zeros followed us to hell and gone," said Davis. One Zero, brasher than the others, came in close and was knocked down.

A third contact with two battleships, heavy cruisers, and destroyers was now reported to the north. The scouting planes attacked, despite the odds.

Now came a mixup. The *Saratoga* had her attack group launched and on the way to the smaller *Ryujo* when the *Enterprise* search planes made contact with the same ship. *Saratoga* pilots bombed the *Ryujo* and lifted it out of the water by several direct hits. When last seen it was dead in the water, burning fiercely and listing heavily. When, following up their contact report, *Enterprise* planes went out to hit the *Ryujo*, they could not find her.

Meanwhile, another *Saratoga* attack group hurt the Jap striking force by hitting the battleships with heavy bombs and the cruiser with at least two torpedoes.

Belatedly, leaving the larger two-carrier Jap force, the *Enterprise* launched two attack groups. Either the large Jap force had retired or was hiding in rain squalls. At any rate it was not found.

The other torpedo plane attack group returned to find the Big E badly wounded.

19. *The Big E Takes It: Solomons*

The last plane of the *Enterprise* attack group had cleared the deck, dipping off the bow with its heavy bomb load and had streaked over the horizon in search of the enemy.

"They'll never make it back," observed an air officer. "In the first place, they won't find their target before dark and in the second, if they do, they'll not be able to return to the carrier. Expendable," he added grimly.

Already the sky was taking on the evening shades of tropical blue and getting ready to be host to a magnificent sunset. When the sky blues up, it is difficult to see small carrier-based planes at high altitude.

Everyone looked long and hard in the direction the Japs were expected. Our scouting planes were returning to the carrier and a typical Jap stunt is to follow a homing scouting plane. During the tenseness, Fighter Pilot Red Brooks radioed: "My section has intercepted a dozen torpedo planes flying low on the water. We are diving on them."

This meant that the Jap dive bombers must be in close. Dive bombers usually precede a torpedo plane attack.

Suddenly keen-eyed Sergeant Schenka of the *Enterprise* Marine detachment shouted: "Here come the bastards."

Everyone strained, imagining they saw, but they didn't.

Then Sergeant Schenka opened fire. On the Big E each gunner has the right to open up on an enemy plane whenever he sees one. His is the responsibility of distinguishing between United States and enemy pilots. Gunnery Officer Lieutenant Commander Lester Livdahl had taught his men to take advantage of the short three seconds available to knock down the Jap before he could unload his bomb.

Sergeant Schenka's 20-mm. gunfire set off the greatest explosive show the *Enterprise* had yet put on. Before the first bomber reached 5,000 feet from its 16,000-foot dive, thousands of tracers from automatic weapons were going into and all around him. Long before—at least a second—the Jap could release his bomb he was out of control and crashed into the sea. But this Jap was quickly followed by a second, then ten, then twenty—all told, forty! At times the air was filled with five Jap dive bombers in a row from 16,000 to 3,000 feet. These forty bombers were escorted by twenty fighters.

The Japs started their attack from the port bow, but as Captain Davis zigzagged the ship violently, they worked around to the starboard bow. Plane after plane was knocked down, their bombs falling wide.

However, the vicious attack could not be stood off entirely. The Japs had a good hard-hitting outfit, and they drove home their attack with concentrated fury. The speed of the attack was tremendously fast—too fast to record—lasting less than four minutes.

Finally an Aichi-99 dive bomber with fixed landing gear came down into a little shallower dive than the rest. He planted his bomb in Group 3 battery, aft of the island structure. Apparently fused with a tenth of a second delay, it exploded below decks, causing considerable material damage.

The bomb, as it slanted through Lieutenant Williamson's battery, started a fire in the powder locker. The young lieutenant at once sized up the situation. He secured the crew of Number 5 gun to fight the fire. Thinking that explosions would follow, he calmly ordered the pharmacist's mate to go forward of the catwalk. "I expect another explosion here and I want you to treat my injured men."

As he shoved the pharmacist's mate away, a Jap plane came in to strafe, with motors screaming above the ear-drum bursting racket of 5-inch shells, anti-aircraft guns, and explosions. The Jap had missed with his bomb. The Jap's fire plowed a furrow down the deck and then through a battery.

One marine was carrying a 20-mm. ammunition drum. A bullet hit and the drum exploded, but miraculously the marine was not killed. Others about him were wounded but the gun kept up its intensive fire.

About one minute—perhaps less—after the first bomb hit in Lieutenant Williamson's compartment, a second Jap bomb hit within 10 feet of the first. Unlike the first, this had an instantaneous bomb fuse and exploded upon contact in the midst of fifty-three men. Of that number forty-one were killed, including Williamson. Men near the explosion were ripped to bits, but those farther away had their clothes ripped off, and were frozen in their working attitudes.

How do American seamen react under fire? Those frozen postures tell the eloquent story. The ship had been hit at the same spot, a minute before. Not a man—save the pharmacist's mate who was ordered and pushed forward—had left his battle station.

One of those dead men was sitting in the pointer seat, leaning into his sights, training his gun on the incoming Jap. The gun was low so the man must have followed him in all the way. Another was straining with a projectile cradled in his empty frozen arms. The heavy projectile had been blown clear and had slammed into a bulkhead which it had dented. A third was handing a powder can to a fourth whose hands were outstretched far, reaching to get it quickly. Such were the naked, burned corpses—a bas-relief one can never forget.

Similar action was going on all over the ship—but of the living one expects it.

Battery Officer Lieutenant E. E. de Garmo of Honolulu had a fragment driven through his foot. He continued firing.

A mount captain received an injury which cost him his eye, but he stayed on his mount to direct its operation and to help supply ammunition despite his bleeding.

He later told me this story, which happened before his injury: "The concussion of the second bomb explosion was terrible. It shook the ship violently. One gunner was blown across the deck from his gun to mine, which he started firing, thinking it was his own. I pointed out his mistake and showed him his own gun, across the flight deck. The marine climbed out, said, 'Pardon me!' and went back to his battery."

Air Group Commander Lou Bauer selected pilots on ability, not rank. "To hell with who they are," he used to say. "I want an honest-to-God flier leading my men into battle."

As a result, two enlisted men—Machinists Eugene Runyan and Red Brooks, had ensigns, lieutenants, and sometimes even lieutenant commanders flying on their wing. On this day Red Brooks, who spotted and reported the Jap torpedo plane attack, and Gene Runyan proved Bauer's theory a good one.

Red's section of four fighters was searching for the Jap dive bombers. At about 14,000 feet his squirrel-shooting eyes picked up a flight of a dozen Jap torpedo planes hugging the water, miles below. At 5,000 feet most pilots would have difficulty seeing them, but not Red. In short order, six of those Japs plowed a furrow into the ocean while the rest, thoroughly disorganized and leaderless, turned tail and fled. That might well have saved the *Enterprise*. It was badly wounded minutes after this action.

While Red Brooks was dispersing these torpedo planes, his buddy Runyan was playing hob with the Jap dive bombers. His four-plane section intercepted the bombers near the carrier. In three minutes, Runyan shot down four in their dives and followed them despite *Enterprise* AA fire. This two-minute flurry raised Gene's bag to eight Jap planes in two engagements—and Fighting Six's total to forty-one.

Not until their chessmen scooted off the board did Ensign James Wyrick and his partner, below decks, know that the Jap attack had begun. For damage control men, who must wait until their ship is injured, chess is a good battle game.

"The ship's radical evolutions made us cuss," said Wyrick, "till I felt the bomb hit and knew I had a large piece of work cut out for me."

He raced to the damaged area. Bomb number two exploded just in front of him and sparkling orange flash, followed by smoke, leaped into the air. With this explosion the powder from the ready box had gone off, killing forty-one of the fifty-three-man crew.

Wyrick found one sailor, knocked punchy by the blast, aimlessly hosing a stream of water into the air although fires were raging near by—out on his feet but still functioning. In passing, Wyrick directed the punchy seaman's hose.

Knowing that the powder below decks was liable to "cook off" by the terrific heat which turned the deck cherry red, Wyrick organized a working party to throw the stuff overboard. Some of those handling the hot powder burned out their palms, but the powder went over the side without interruption.

Then a third bomb ripped out a section of the flight deck, started a large fire below. Before the fire gained headway, a near miss shot a column of tons of water, some of which drained through the flight deck hole and helped control the fire below.

That same column of water carried off a man. Just before the deluge, this wounded man with arm and leg gone pleaded with shipmates to throw him overboard: "I'm finished." Men refused. Unnoticed, he pulled himself foot by foot to the ship's side and from here the water carried him off.

20. *Steering Room Aft*

When the first Jap bomb exploded, it carried away the ventilating trunk leading to the steering room aft where there were seven men deep in the ship near the propellers. Instead of fresh air, the blower at once delivered a deluge of Foamite, used in fighting the fires, and boiling water which had run over the hot decks. Repair parties quickly secured the ventilation shafts and closed the overhead valves. Thus seven men—four engineers and three quartermasters—were hermetically sealed in the smoke-filled steering-gear room.

Alexander Paul Trymofiew, twenty-seven, a husky chief electrician's mate, was one of those men.

"At first we did not worry," he said. "We just kept flattened out, expecting a Jap torpedo attack. A man can't stand to worry when he's dogged down—it would drive him nuts.

"It was hot to begin with. During General Quarters, when we are secured for battle, the normal temperature of our station is 120 degrees. We could stand that fine, because we were used to daily G.Q.

"But it got hotter. When no one was looking, I snatched some quick looks and saw the thermometer climb to 140 degrees Fahrenheit, then 150, 155, and then 160. The added heat," Trymofiew explained, "was due to the closing of all exhaust vents of our electric motors and the fire burning in the compartment above us.

"I was the only one who really knew how hot it was, and I did not tell a man.

"At 160 degrees my heavy sweating stopped and I started drying up. When my skin dried it pulled tight. Moving my muscles was like cracking broiled skin after twelve hours on the beach. Every time I took a breath of hot air it burned through. From the outside, a hot magnet seemed to be sucking up all my moisture.

"We had a gallon jug of warm water among us, but every time we drank, we'd throw up foamy-like matter. At the same time I had no control over my bladder and I was too weak to relieve myself properly.

"My main concern was fresh air. There was that clear driving thought: 'I've got to get fresh air to keep going.'

"Up to the time we were ordered to abandon station, we had no thought of leaving. We knew that the ship depended on us, and we knew that the Lucky E would get us out again as she had often enough before.

"Then Chief Machinist Smith called us by phone and told us what screws to get out of a ventilator shaft to get air. I tried but was too weak, and I gave up and quit.

"We didn't talk. Talking took effort.

"I didn't realize how far gone I was until I dropped my empty pipe. My mind told me to pick it up and I couldn't.

"It kept getting hotter. The electric motor was heating the air still more in our small compartment and drawing what little fresh air we had left from the crowded room. I crawled into the small adjoining rudder room. On the way I took my last look at the thermometer and saw it was 170 degrees. I got my head into the rudder well where bilgewater usually collects and found it slightly cooler.

"My eyeballs were stinging hot. Then black spots played in front of them and my body refused to obey my will. From there on I don't remember much. . . ."

The first Jap attack was over but an even greater battle for the ship's life was about to commence. Jap planes were reported near. Fires were still burning—on a ship which carried high octane gasoline, torpedoes, bombs, and ammunition. Again the life of the ship depended upon the individual efforts of a few men.

Still steaming away from the scene of attack with fires raging, the *Enterprise* suddenly keeled into hard rudder right, turning in tight circles and helpless. The steering engine, where the seven men were trapped, was out. Then sounded that dreaded signal: "Steering control is away from the bridge."

In the steering room only one man, William N. Marcoux of Bay City, Michigan, was still conscious despite the terrific heat. He had moved but little, saving himself.

"When I heard that siren, asking that steering control be returned from us to the bridge," he said, "I knew it my duty to start the auxiliary unit. I remember dragging myself to the control board. I kept telling myself that the Big E depended on me—I was the last man left who counted."

When Marcoux got halfway through the comparatively

simple task, fate interceded. He slipped to the hot steel cat-walk unconscious.

Under the able direction of Lieutenant Commander Carl Yost, the assistant engineer, the ship was doing something to get the seven men out, and more important, to restore the ship's steering. Everyone knew that there were at least two and perhaps three large Jap carriers within striking distance, able to deal a blow even more crippling and concentrated than that which had been delivered less than two hours before.

Repair parties following Commander Yost's instructions were battling furiously to make their way to steering aft. Numerous men who attempted to get through the wreckage-blocked, smoke-filled room with various types of rescue breathing apparatus were overcome with heat and had to be hauled out unconscious by safety lines.

On the *Enterprise's* bridge, Captain Davis called upon one of his warrant officers—Chief Machinist Smith. (Smith had enlisted in the Navy years earlier at sixteen, stretching his years to the required eighteen for the records.) Captain Davis simply asked Chief Machinist Smith to see what he could do. "Do you know the steering gear installation? Then do your stuff the best you can. It's time for the *Enterprise* to go!"

Smith replied: "I'll go."

On the first attempt, Smith got halfway through the wreckage-strewn compartment before he was overcome with heat. He was revived with artificial respiration. He then attempted a different route. This time he got almost to the hatch before fainting. Restored a second time, Smith, in company with Cecil S. Robinson, fought down to the steering-gear room. He was annoyed to find that *the seven men had disappeared!*

Smith worked as fast as the heat permitted. He saw that the Foamite and water from the fire fighters had stopped one unit. He got the standby unit running and then restored steering control to the bridge. For the time being, the *Enterprise* again steered a straight course.

But Smith continued. He tore away the ventilating trunk leading to the standby unit he had started, so that no further water or Foamite could enter. This took an added five minutes in the overheated chamber. Then he ripped away some of the blocked ventilation shafts to cool the room and keep the motors functioning. In doing this, he found where the seven trapped men had attempted to disconnect the blower but had been able to remove only one screw. He wondered about the absence of the men, but was too busy with his job of getting things under control to investigate.

By this time the heat had risen beyond 180 degrees, and Smith suffered the weakening effects of dehydration. His knees wanted to fold. The heat drew the strength from his very marrow.

Immediately upon getting out, Smith became unconscious. He remembers that he wanted his hands to pull the mask from his face but they refused. He was just too tired. Revived for the third time, Smith reported to Captain Davis and informed him that he had control over his ship. "I will keep the control on the bridge as long as it is humanly possible, sir."

The Captain's relief was evident. The greater, because *Enterprise* search planes had located and reported a large Jap torpedo attack force within ten minutes of the helpless ship.

After the report, Smith went to the hangar deck and heaved without letup for many minutes. Recovered from his vomiting, he returned to the steering room. This time he ripped away more ventilation shafts. The room was cooler now. He thought to look at the thermometer and the mer-

cury column was near the top, just above the last mark regis-
tering 180 degrees.

On his next trip, the third, Smith saw that the excessive
heat had affected the machinery and had caused the grease to
melt off the large rudder shafts. This in itself would have put
the machinery out of commission again within a half-hour's
operation, according to Commander Yost. Smith immediately
greased the large plungers attached to the rudder yoke.
When the room cooled, Smith refused to leave the steering
room for twenty-four hours.

Two days later the Big E was steaming for Pearl Harbor,
her rudder sensitive to any order from the bridge. Many men
had been given to the sea, among whom was Robert H.
Williams, one of the seven who had not survived the steering
room ordeal.

Trymofiew had lost eighteen pounds, and his friends
scarcely recognized his drawn face. He could not drink
enough water.

But Commander Yost was puzzled. How did those seven
men get out of that sealed compartment, through the debris
and up to the hangar deck? Chief Machinist Smith told him
definitely that they were not in the small steering room when
he went below. Yost knew that those seven men were unconscious or too weak to get out under their own power.

The Commander went from man to man among those who
could have been there. "Do you know anything about how
the seven men got out of the steering room?"

The reply was always "No, sir." He went to the six men.
"All we know, sir, is that we came to on the hangar deck."

Finally, after asking forty men, Commander Yost came to
Ernest Richard Visto, a large slow-moving blond Swede from
the Middle West.

Visto disclaimed having been in the steering room but his

manner was so evasive that Commander Yost persisted. "You left your battle station to help, Visto. Where did you go?"

Then with some reluctance Visto admitted: "I'm sorry, sir. I left my station when I thought I could help out. I couldn't make one of those fancy breathing masks fit me, so I went in with my gas mask even though I was breaking orders. I worked my way down and I guess I got them out. I'm sorry, sir, that I left my battle station."

Yost demanded: "Do you mean to tell me, Visto, that you got those seven men out alone?"

Visto nodded.

"And you fought your way through all that wreckage while others couldn't, and that in spite of the terrific heat you lifted those seven men out alone?"

"Well, I did have to lug and shove them around, more or less."

"And did you become unconscious?"

Visto looked ashamed.

"After I got the last man out, I went hazy in my head and passed out. And that's another thing, I guess, I shouldn't have done."

21. *Then There Were Four*

The moon rose and the sea was filled with its light. Peace descended over the torn, bruised ship. The ship's company knew that their guns had been silenced and much equipment immobilized. They knew of the havoc in the chief's quarters. They saw their three doctors working over the seriously wounded. A large number were dead. They knew that due to Lieutenant Spear's work the holes blown through the hull around the waterline had been shored up.

They knew, but they did not talk of death. They talked of the superb gunnery. They compared this sixty-plane attack with the five-plane attack in the Marshalls, back in February.

They sobered when they saw that two torpedo planes, one dive bomber and two fighters failed to return but rejoiced when they learned that Caldwell and his ten dive bomber pilots were not missing but had gone on to Guadalcanal.

In contrast, they reckoned the Jap planes shot down—approximately eighty. A hasty tabulation showed that their fighter planes got about twenty-seven; the ship's gunners about fifteen, the escorting screen AA about nine, with six more probables. The companion carrier got about eighteen, while many of the remaining Jap planes—as usual—were deserted by their carriers and seen to crash into the water without fuel.

There was exultation too as the *Enterprise* set her course for the east. "Now," said the sailors, "we're headed for the mainland and a repair job."

Few hit their sacks early. Sweaty and tired, they gathered among the parked planes on the gently rising and falling deck and talked with intimacy born of battle. Officers and men were close—each knew he could depend on the other. The tremendous strain of the Jap waters was about to end, for the time being.

To keep their minds off friends killed, they talked of crazy incidents:

One man had a bottle of milk spill on him and shouted: "I'm wounded! There's blood running all up and down my spine!"

Supply Officer Fox, in charge of the mess boys, told how one of them reported to the sick bay: "Boss, I'm sick plumb through from my kidney on up to my temples and my arms don't want to work none. I can hardly lift them up to here." Painfully and slowly he lifted them elbow high.

"How high could you lift them before the battle?"

"Oh, I could lift them clear up to here," he said, lifting them high above his head.

A communications officer told how during the height of the attack one man carefully combed his hair. A second took up a broom and cleaned his station.

Down in the engine room, Lieutenant Commander Yost recalled: "A boy heard the telephone jingle. He answered: 'Start talking, man; it's your nickel.' The man was the ship's captain."

The executive officer, Commander Boone, told how, when the last wave of Jap planes came in, and the loudspeaker announced that twenty-four enemy bombers were approaching the ship's stern, "A sailor in my station, aft, shouted: 'Call the chaplain.' "

There was a surge of renewed confidence in the ship and in shipmates. This time the *Enterprise* proved that she could take it no matter how tough the going; and the men proved that from fighter pilots 15,000 feet up to the steering gear boys deep in the ship, they were magnificent in combat.

Yet, after hasty repairs in Pearl Harbor, the *Enterprise* crew was to look back on this attack as merely a bush league game.

Not long after, the carrier death knell sounded again. This time it was the *Wasp*. She was one of our two newest carriers, having been commissioned as recently as April, 1940. On duty in the South Seas in support of a transport force headed for Guadalcanal, the *Wasp* was struck by torpedoes on September 15. It was early afternoon when she was hit, but it was not until nightfall that she sank, sent to the bottom by our own destroyers when hope was abandoned that she could be brought under control.

The Japs were exerting every nerve and sinew in effort to exterminate our carrier forces. The *Lexington*, the *York-*

town, the *Wasp*—the toll was already three. They had tried mightily to add the Big E to their score, but they had failed. We now had four major carriers; not all of them could be in the Pacific at one time. Those that were would have to share the ever-growing burden of defending the long, thin Pacific battlefront till help could come in the shape of new, big carriers from our shipyards. The help was not to come that year. The *Enterprise* tightened its belt. The line must be held at all costs.

5

OCTOBER 25 – OCTOBER 26

22. *Eleven at Henderson Field*

Eleven dive bomber pilots from the *Enterprise*, led by Lieutenant Turner F. Caldwell, Jr., helped to change the fate of Guadalcanal.

It was luck that they got into the air that August 24. The Japs unloosed their crippling attack on the carrier just as the last of the eleven got into the air with their 1,000-pound bombs. They made their rendezvous during the attack and were sitting in the air waiting for orders. Some of the pilots frankly thought it was their last flight. It was going to be dark within two hours. Only three of them had ever made a night landing.

With the position of the Jap ships reported, the order came: "Proceed to the enemy and attack." The fliers went 60 miles beyond the reported position searching for the Japs and by doing so endangered their return gas supply. Nonetheless they failed to find the Jap fleet.

Two choices now remained for Caldwell: attempt a return to the carrier or proceed to Henderson Field. Neither choice was easy. The fate of the field was uncertain, since the Japs had raked it with heavy shell fire the night before. The terrain was unfamiliar. There was probably little food.

On the other hand, if he set a course to where the carrier

ought to be, the planes might never reach it. Also, assuming that by luck their gas should hold out and their search prove fruitful, there was no guarantee that the carrier would be able to land them. What damage had the ship suffered from the Jap attack?

Turner knew that Guadalcanal was very short on air power. Should he risk having these badly needed planes land in the water or should he risk taking them to Henderson Field? He opened up on the air and called his men: "We are going to Guadalcanal."

This was August 24. If Caldwell had known how really desperate the need of air support was at Henderson he would have hesitated even less. We took the field on August 7. Ten days later, on August 17, my friend Richard Tregaskis was writing in his diary: * "We are still without air support—and, if the Japs only knew it, pretty much at the mercy of sea or air attack. . . . We are hoping very hard that our planes will arrive before the Japs do." Two days later he was still writing: "We went back to sleep to the accompaniment of 'grousing' about the fact that we on Guadalcanal had not yet received any air support." Finally the next afternoon—August 20—Marine fighter and dive bomber planes arrived. "It seemed almost unbelievable," says Tregaskis, "that we did not have to dive for shelter at the sound."

Caldwell ordered his pilots to jettison their bombs, in order to stretch what fuel remained, and the men flew in total darkness to a field none of them had seen before. As they approached, Caldwell signaled that they were friendly. The field personnel put out a few light pots. The first two Big E pilots landed downwind, hedge-hopped dimly outlined wrecks on the field and avoided bomb craters. The remainder came in the right way, and also missed some thirty-odd wrecks on the field and landed without accident.

* *Guadalcanal Diary*, by Richard Tregaskis, Random House, 1943.

These Big E fliers were the first carrier pilots to operate against the enemy from land. Their small force almost doubled the planes at the field. One marine told them: "You are bringing us the hope of re-enforcements. That's what we need here."

These are the eleven men who flew their planes until only one was left and helped stop three Jap invasion attempts:

Ensign Elmer E. Liffner, about twenty-four, had very blue eyes and the lean face that all carrier pilots, even the heavy ones, seem to have. Constant flying beats out the fat and takes out the slack and what you have left is mostly skin and bones. "Liff" was decorated for a little job of destruction on a Jap carrier during Midway and he carried his citation even to Guadalcanal. The fellows ribbed him: "Liff, it looks like you have to prove you're a hero with papers." Liff was married just a month before he joined the carrier and his big topic was his wife. With the rest he would wind up wondering if he'd ever see her again. Liff lost more than twenty-five pounds and his five foot eleven looked very thin. The men compared belts and made bets about who was losing the most weight and Liff would always win. Before it was over he had eight spare inches of belt.

Ensign Walter W. Coolbaugh was from Pennsylvania, near Scranton. Nothing ever scared Coolbaugh, and he was one of the wildest and most reckless of the group. For example, none of the boys liked night flying except Coolbaugh. And while at Guadalcanal he always wanted to drop flares on Jap ships just to scare hell out of them. He would strafe heavy Jap men-of-war with his two puny .50's. He was always having close calls and he always came out right side up and walking. He used to kid the others about their "just dying" to get back to one girl. "Follow me in, boys, and I'll find you a sweetheart near every airport."

Coolbaugh's roommate aboard ship was Lieutenant (j.g.) Harold Buell of Ottumwa, Iowa. They were of one size and traded clothes. Hal came the closest to being the kid of the outfit, and looked less than seventeen. When in port, the happy-go-lucky pair were always the first off at the beach and always came back at the very last minute. Buell never tired of whipping out his girl's picture. After eight months of flying in combat (he started in the Coral Sea battle and was still flying at the close of the first year of war) he worried: "I'm almost afraid to go back—if I do—because I've changed such a lot. I'll just bet she won't have me." He carried everything in the book to ward off bad luck. He had a four-leaf clover, a rabbit's foot, a good-luck ring, coins. He wore a cross, explaining: "If I go down on a South Sea island I want the natives to think I'm a Christian." On that same chain he wore a little box with a pair of dice—seven up. "That's to shoot craps for the cannibal chief's pants." But the best luck, he claimed, was in his pilot license folder—his girl's picture.

Another Iowa boy was Ensign Elmer Conzett. He was about twenty-five, tall and thin with a firm, pointed chin, a narrow face and crispy black hair and said about five words at a time, even about home and his folks. When he did say his piece, the others paid attention.

The biggest of the eleven was Ensign Lloyd W. Barker, appropriately from the West Coast. He looked big and nervy, and was. Once he and young Buell dove on a Jap ship. Returning from their two-man-wave attack they met a four-motored Jap bomber, as big as a Flying Fortress, with a crew of ten. Barker started the aggressive fight; Hal's guns were jammed. Cruising along behind, Buell noticed that Barker was only using one gun and had to fire, charge, and shoot because they were "on the fritz" too. "Come on, you finish him," Barker called to Buell over the radio. "I have no front guns," Buell informed him. With that Barker and Buell decided to break off the engagement with the frantically dodging Jap plane.

Shortest was Ensign Walter Brown who carried a strong Maine accent wherever he went. Brownie was a good kid, no drinking and no smoking. He was the nearest to being openly religious about his way of life than any of them. They all got religion before they got out of Guadalcanal. When others might talk about their conquests, Brownie would somehow sneak in a few fine words about Bucksport, Maine. He talked about its scenery, its climate, its potatoes that he missed at Guadalcanal, the snow and the trout fishing and woodcock hunting. It was downright dangerous to let him get started, because his longing for the mountains made the men want to bawl.

The expression: "Well, this is it!" fitted Ensign Harold Manford. He was a big fellow when they went in but he lost 35 pounds and it left his frame bony. He kept saying: "I'm not the man I used to be and I don't think I ever will be." During slack hours Buck would tell the boys about movie stars he had known in Hollywood. Also Buck did not mind telling them he was from California. The only injury he collected was one night during a Jap bombardment when he jumped into a shell hole. Suddenly the sky fell atop him. Next day he had a black eye where the marine's boot had landed. "Now, if I were in the Army, I'd have me a Purple Heart," he said dryly.

"Never-Miss-'Em" Fink (Chris Fink of Grey Bull, Wyoming) was the German-looking man of the outfit. He was six feet with a rugged makeup. He spoke German well and used to tell the fellows that if he got shot down over Jap territory, he'd give them a "Heil, Hitler!" and stick to the story that he was a Nazi until they proved him otherwise. Fink knew that he was better than any Jap. That was part of his whole being. He wouldn't let anyone run over him, and yet everyone liked him.

Lieutenant (j.g.) T. T. Guillory was called "The Little Hard-Hitter." Gill got that nickname when a medical officer at Guadalcanal was looking for him. "I don't know what the man's name is," the doctor said, "but I'm looking for your little hard hitter." Gill was shot down in Midway after hitting a Jap carrier. A Catalina picked him up.

Second in command of the men was Lieutenant Roger Woodhull, the "Exec," about twenty-eight, chunky, broad-shouldered, with a firm mouth, and close-cropped hair. He was well mannered and mild. But that could fool you. He was a good man in a plane and a good leader. Woodhull had been married only a month before he left for the Pacific. Like the others he wondered: "Will she know me?" Roger got sick and lost a lot of weight but still there was never a time when he wouldn't give all he had to see a job done.

Finally there was the Skipper, Turner Caldwell. In the air the boys called him Stinky. The Skipper did not look unlike General Grant when his beard blossomed. He knew no fear although he was small—about five feet six, and slight—about 135 pounds. His hair was sandy, light brown, his eyes blue. The Skipper was always considerate of his men. They talked with him about sweethearts, families, or episodes which had left scars in their past. And in turn his pilots would never let him down. Every man was willing to do everything he could for the Skipper. He made them feel that they were Navy men and that what they did was in their line of duty. For example, he did not recommend that his ten men receive Navy decorations; it was simply their duty. The Navy meant much to Caldwell; his father had also been an Academy man.

When the men are asked: "How in hell did you go

through those hardships at Guadalcanal?" they will tell you: "It was Caldwell. He made us believe it was a privilege."

Marines hurriedly gathered about the small re-enforcement when it landed and rejoiced that more planes had come. Even though there was little chow and it was late, they hustled the boys some food and then bunked them down on blood-stained stretchers after showing the *Enterprise* pilots the nearest dugout trench "just in case . . ." The pilots had just gotten to sleep when the Japs began to shell them with naval guns. This was to happen almost nightly.

Buell said: "Coolbaugh and I left our stretchers and broke for the dugout. There were already a couple of casualties. About every night five men or more were killed. But more awful, we found we could not sleep. Guadalcanal was about ten times as bad as a plane. You couldn't fight back, although the Marines would shoot with even their .45's."

After the shelling, Woodhull, Coolbaugh, and Brown volunteered to go after the Jap surface ships and strafe them. Only these three had night-flying experience. It was semi-darkness with a quarter moon. They found the Jap ships and bombed them. Not satisfied with that, the three dove upon them repeatedly and strafed them. From the land the watchers could see the dive bombers' two little gun bursts spitting defiance into the Japs' ships while every Jap ship blasted back its terrific reply.

Coming back, Brown got separated from the other two. He realized that he was lost and flew along the land hoping that he might keep in the air until daylight. His gas held until there was enough light in the sky to help him make a forced landing on another island's beach.

Everyone felt despondent about Brown—he was a big item in their team. They would miss his talk of Bucksport. "Why did it have to happen to him? He was the cleanest thinking and living man in our outfit."

Early next morning, the Japs returned the compliment and strafed the boys at the "Pagoda," a small 30- by 30-foot Japanese temple with dipping eaves which they had erected during their stay. The strafing indicated that the Japs knew that the "Pagoda" was being used for flight operations head-quarters.

That day the action continued. A Jap transport force was reported and the *Enterprise* pilots (minus Brown) went out and hit it. The liner was loaded with several thousand troops —having made the short haul from Rabaul. The transport, flying an army flag and crowded with troops, was hit time and again. Fired, it burned the rest of the day. As a result of this action by Caldwell and his men, the Jap occupation force turned tail and headed north—and Guadalcanal for the present was saved, for the 20,000-ton vessel had carried more troops than there were Marines on the island.

Brown's wrecked plane was sighted two days later by one of his fellow fliers. He flew over it low and made out a native in Brown's gear sitting in it big as life while around the plane were fully a hundred others. The supposition, of course, was that poor Brown had been captured by cannibals.

Fourteen days later, when a couple of amphibian planes had been added to the force at Guadalcanal, one of the pilots went out to investigate Brown's fate, prepared for the worst.

He found Brown dining on fried chicken, native vege-tables, pork, and milk. He even told of eating fried eggs—while at Guadalcanal his fellow fliers were living on Jap-left food, some of it wormy, and would gladly have paid ten dol-lars for one fried egg.

Brown's story was this: Island missionaries had instructed natives that planes with white stars were friendly and those with red balls were bad. And they told natives to bring all

white-starred pilots to the priest. In return for the fine treatment, Brown explained, "I gave the native my flying gear.
How those women went for the silk parachute! It's instinct
with women to want silk pants."

"And we thought you had been eaten . . ." growled his
"rescuer."

The pilots were to learn, and soon, that flying was the
least of their new job. They had also to gas their planes. Gas
was conveyed by captured Jap trucks, and it had to be handled in drums and hand-pumped for hours and hours. It is no
small matter to handle fifty gallons, but this multiplied many
times makes the work deadly and the hours unending. Then
there was the long tedious job of replacing worn and shot-up
parts from junked and wrecked planes. But these pilots soon
learned the routine.

The first thing in the morning, they'd gas the dirty dust-
covered planes. After that came the bombs—and to handle
heavy bombs without the proper equipment is no lark. The
men thought with longing of the efficient crews of the Big E
who gave them motor-perfect planes, gassed and armed,
ready to take off.

Determined on getting the field and driving the Americans
into the sea, the persistent Japs sent another invasion force
within two days. This time it was a stronger one.

Again, *Enterprise* dive bombers were ready—five of the ten
taking off to make the attack while the remainder got their
planes ready for a second follow-up assault wave.

When the first five returned from their attack, Caldwell
and Fink reported hits on the enemy ships. Never-Miss-'Em
Fink hit a large transport smack in the middle. The sides
blew right out and she exploded and burst into enormous
flames and sank at once. Another transport and a cruiser and
two smaller ships, presumably destroyers, were hit. Caldwell
told the five pilots that he thought it quite likely that the

second transport was sunk and the cruiser left dead in the water—and Caldwell was never one for overstatement.

The second wave of *Enterprise* planes found the tell-tale oil slick left by the damaged cruiser and tracked it thirty miles. When they found the cruiser, Barker and Buell dove on it almost together.

"As we dove," reported Buell, "the Jap skipper wrapped his ship into a tight turn. As he was turning, the AA fire poured up." However, undeterred, the two went down, released their bombs at 2,000 feet and as they pulled up and banked sharp to look, they saw a fire they had started. A near miss from a third plane rocked the ship. (Near misses sometimes open the sides of a ship; for instance, practically all depth charge damage is done by near misses.)

Buell and Barker moaned all the way back because they had not seen the ship sink.

That night in the "Pagoda," the *Enterprise* bag was computed: one 20,000-ton transport sunk, a second large transport hit, one cruiser badly hit and left dead in the water, one destroyer hit and believed badly damaged. More important, a second Jap invasion attempt—ships again carrying at least twice as many troops as we had Marines on the island—was turned back.

The third day after the Jap transport invasion excitement died down, the pilots got their first taste of Japanese high altitude bombing which was to become daily fare. Search planes would report the approaching enemy. The alarm given, the pilots would make a wild scramble to their planes, crank them, jump into them, wait in line, and take off as fast as possible to get their slow planes from 10 to 20 miles away to be comparatively safe from Zero danger. Then they watched the fight between the Marine fighters and the enemy.

As they raced off the junk-covered field at 70 miles an

hour, occasionally one of the pilots would slip into a bomb hole trying to dodge other larger bomb craters. Besides, they had to watch for old wreckage. "God, if we only just had a tow car to get these wrecks out of our way," the marines would moan. And each time the boys took off they wouldn't know if there would be a field to come back to.

However, they *could* count on the Marines. Before the Jap planes were out of sight the Marines would be back on the dusty field with shovels, frantically filling up the holes so the pilots could land with comparative safety.

When our scouting planes failed to report the coming Japs, it was bad. Then the Japs would catch our planes on the ground, and in this manner three *Enterprise* planes were lost.

On one attack, the pilots' first, twenty-one Jap bombers escorted by twenty fighter planes roared in—a force which clearly outnumbered the planes the Americans had. However, up went our Marine fighters to give battle and they took a big chunk out of the enemy, shooting down eight bombers and six Zero fighters. Two of our men were badly shot up. One succeeded in making a dead-stick landing. The other was lost.

After this attack, the carrier boys permitted themselves to wonder if they were ever going back to the nice clean comfortable carrier where they belonged. Cool-headed Skipper Caldwell summed up the sentiment: "The Marines need dive bombers here. We might just as well stay for a while. The Japs want this place and they want it bad. Our forces must hold Guadalcanal if we are to hold the South Pacific. We can do our best work here." That settled it.

A few days later the *Enterprise* boys had just finished evening chow—their second meal of the day, because food was scarce and the Japs had a nasty habit of raiding between 11:30 A.M. and 1:30 P.M.—when two of their scouts, Barker and Liffner, sent in a message reporting contact with four Jap ships—one light cruiser and three destroyers. Five men, Caldwell, Buell, Coolbaugh, Fink, and Conzett, hustled off. As they did so, the scouts amplified their report: "We have just attacked and hit one of their ships. She is slowing up. We are still over them." He gave the Jap position 65 miles away. An hour of daylight, enough to do the job quickly and get back, remained.

The carrier boys found the ships and Caldwell opened up. "This is Stinky. We have spotted the ships and are going in on them."

A Marine flier, commanding another group, said: "O.K., we'll follow you boys in."

The Big E boys peeled off. Caldwell smacked the damaged cruiser. Fink, second, got a direct hit on a destroyer. Meanwhile, the Jap ships had turned from east to north and began throwing heavy AA, bouncing the incoming planes. Conzett and Buell went down side by side on the third ship. As their 500-pounders hit a destroyer amidships, there were two large explosions followed by several smaller explosions and fires spread rapidly. Never-Miss-'Em Fink's big 1,000-pound bomb had split his destroyer in half and she was now sinking rapidly.

Marine pilots administered the finishing blows. One Marine, Lieutenant Mitchell, to prevent the Japs from abandoning their sinking ships, dove down to strafe. He alone failed to return.

Later, a plane flying over the area reported only one crippled Jap ship afloat. And yet Skipper Caldwell recommended no man for a decoration——this was all in the line of duty.

Day and night and night and day it was the same story.

Less a menace than a nightmarish nuisance, "Maytag Charlie," a lone Jap marauder, visited nightly and dropped occasional bombs and flares. Exhausted men could not sleep, wondering if his flares would be followed by bombers. One Sunday night, August 30, twenty bombers did follow, and when those bombs were through rocking the earth the Japs began a terrifying bombardment from the sea.

Several pilots managed to get their planes into the air, including Conzett who took off with Major Brown of the Marines to bomb and strafe the Jap ships. But clouds settled quickly and the ceiling dropped to zero. Brown and Conzett flew low, not more than 750 feet, over two Jap warships without seeing them. When they were overhead, the Japs suddenly opened up.

Spike Conzett heard the shell whack as it hit the floor board and then strike him in the back of the leg and lodge in his shin bone. A Jap 20-mm. shell makes a hole big enough to ram three fingers through. Even then Conzett managed to pull off and make good his escape.

But flying through the heavy clouds, together with his loss of blood, befuddled Spike. He went out a long distance in the soup and then tried to work back to Henderson Field. But every time he tried to come back the Japs opened up. "Then I got scared," he said. "After three times my nerve left me. I knew I was losing blood. But finally it came to me that I'd better get altitude. I don't know why it didn't come to me before. When I got up to 8,000 feet a 5-inch Jap shell burst near me and my plane went into a spin."

This might have been the end of Spike's story but the fellow kept his head. He recovered, and by pulling his head into his cockpit and flying by instruments alone, he came out of the spin and down on the other side of Guadalcanal. His plight there was equally bad—completely separated from the field and wounded. Lost, Spike flew almost an hour trying to figure his position. Then, just before the field men decided to black out, Spike saw the lights. As he approached, jeep drivers turned on headlights and Conzett brought his ship in and was lifted out of his plane.

The eleven had little to eat. For a while bread was a luxury. When the boys came they had only Jap food to eat—consisting of wormy rice, jerked beef, Jap candy packaged like American caramels. There were Japanese officers' cigarettes, mild and not bad.

It was some time before fresh meat was brought in. When it came, there was enough chicken for only 300 men. The mess cooks had a big drawing to see who'd get the chicken and the aviation mess cook was lucky. It was the big event of their stay—and the chicken was fried in big pieces, a half a chicken at a time.

One of the *Enterprise* fliers had just returned from a flight and had gone for his hunk of fried chicken, when the Jap bombers came. He grabbed the chicken, hot as it was, and raced with it in his shirt to the dugout. "No Jap's going to come between me and my chicken," he said, eating happily while bombs dropped.

Fortunately the Japs had started a filtering system on Guadalcanal so there was water, though warm. If anyone had brought an iced drink into the hot tepid jungle, or a coke, the stuff would easily have sold for ten bucks a bottle. As it was, I saw a fifth of "Cream of Kentucky" Bourbon auctioned for $150.

Along with the bad food, most of the men got dysentery. Once off their feed it was hard to get back again, and once sick, one couldn't keep food down. "It was eat and puke," said Fink. All of them lost weight.

In addition to bombing, the nightly shelling gave them no peace. No matter how often it came, it filled men with horrible dread. You can't get used to it. One early morning, after a sleepless night, Turner and his boys got fighting mad and took off and happily found a Jap sub unloading troops and supplies. They bombed it. Then they went back to bed and, emotions relieved, slept soundly.

On the night of September 12 came a real shelling. Everything they had gone through before was play. This lasted for hours. Yet finally when it was over, all the Big E men were still alive. Each one felt his prayer had saved him.

However, peace was not theirs. The Japs were using delayed fuses; shells were exploding eleven hours after firing ceased. And then, when the eleven hours were over, all were taut, expecting others to go off.

The men tried to time their flights so they would not be in the air during malaria fever attacks. But this would not always work out. As a result one marine who saw his malaria-suffering friend fly into the water, became unbalanced. And his condition obviously affected everyone who flew.

But along with the hope for re-enforcements, replacements, and new planes, there were horseplay and practical jokes and new verses to add to "From the Halls of Montezuma," such as:

> Now when Gabriel toots his mighty flute,
>   calling old campaigners home,
> And Tojo's —— hang on the walls
>   of Valhalla's golden dome,
> Then the Lord will wink at Vandergrift, while
>   he's eating Spam and beans,
> Sayin': "God on High sees eye to eye with
>   United States Marines. . . ."

Then too when times got dull, for example, one could always get up a party to go Jap souvenir hunting. Marines were good at it.

One afternoon, the Marines made an advance of about 400 yards. A Jap counterattack that night drove them back. However, next morning a group of souvenir hunters came for their loot and found the Japs entrenched with their dead. It made the hunters boiling mad. "The bastards can't rob us like this," they decided, and launched a spirited, unscheduled, unofficered counterattack and drove the Japs well back and got their campaign flags, Jap money, pistols, rifles, and knives.

But under it all was the stern reality of the situation. "Re-enforcements are not coming. What will we do if the Japs take over?" All of the pilots had their minds made up to go into the hills and fight it out in guerrilla action, and the Big E fliers spent hours preparing and filling jungle kits with "iron" rations, ammunition, and medical supplies.

The number three *Enterprise* plane lost was Buell's. It was just a little after midnight. The Japs were shelling and Hal, although not a night-trained pilot, was damned tired of just taking it. Taking off, his plane pulled to the left. Buell tried to keep from crashing but it pulled off the runway and went out of control. Suddenly he saw two parked planes looming up. To save those planes was now the all-important thing. He gave his plane gas, pulled back and hurdled the plane into the air 20 feet, saving them. But as he came down a cap-tured Jap steam roller was dead ahead. He gave it a glancing blow, shearing the motor off his plane and leaving his feet sticking out in front. Then the wheels collapsed and the plane stopped just after Hal's heavy bomb reeled off. Behind him, the motor which had been sheared off burst into flame. His own oil lines were broken and he himself was covered with oil and a fire would have meant cremation. But Hal's only injury was a cut on his eyelid from a piece of his jammed goggles.

Short of planes, the pilots busied themselves with various chores. They washed their sweaty, dust-weighted clothes in a river about a mile from Henderson Field, and looked at the Japs on the other side. Here they swam and soaped with highly perfumed Jap soap, and washed their Jap underwear consisting of breech cloth, socks, and cotton pants and shirts.

One day Buell and Caldwell were out on a log well into the river, washing, and got the scare of their lives. The two naked men didn't see the Jap planes until they were almost directly overhead. They hugged the log as the brown mahogany-colored planes swooped low. Bombs dropped within 100 feet of the huddling men who feared to get in the water, as it is nearly always fatal to be in water when a bomb explodes near by. After the bombs exploded and the planes were gone, Buell walked along the beach barefooted. Suddenly he jumped and yelled with pain. It was only a hot fragment about the size of his little finger and they laughed about that one a long time.

At the same time at Henderson Field, Fink and Brown were caught in their planes on the ground. They ducked into a ditch which fifteen seconds later was straddled by heavy bombs. They were lifted four feet and dropped down flat with fragments dropping all around and buried with dirt. For three hours Fink couldn't hear. In near-by holes, five marines never got up.

Next day, the Japs came again. One of the *Enterprise* planes was hit and its fire spread to others and then into ammunition boxes. As these boxes exploded, pieces dropped over the flier's camp and for an hour no one dared move until the entire dump was expended.

Like a cracked record the story goes on repeating itself: Guadalcanal was shelled again. This time for two hours by five destroyers and one cruiser. Searching for them next day with a vengeance, Woodhull, Coolbaugh, and Brown located three destroyers and cruisers. After debating on how to attack with their dive bombers through heavy clouds, Coolbaugh, the wild man, said: "God damn the bastards, I'll blow them out of the sea." So saying, he climbed for an attack through the clouds. As he came in, he went into an inverted spin—a flier's worst enemy, from which few come out alive. Before he knew what was up, his canteen which was tied to his seat began hitting him in the face and he realized that he was upside down with his bomb on. Rolling out of that one, he held his bomb as long as he could and released it. And of all the lucky shots made in this war, Coolbaugh's will be the luckiest. It was a direct hit on a destroyer and blew several holes in his plane because he was in too close.

Early in September, *Enterprise* scouts returned from the Santa Isabel sector with a curious tale. They said they found a hundred barges camouflaged with trees and scrubs, apparently the makings of another invasion attempt. Using this camouflage the Japs apparently were attempting to sneak in to Guadalcanal.

These one hundred barges were tailor-made targets for bombs and .50-caliber machine guns.

Skipper Caldwell, Fink, Coolbaugh, and Manford went first. They found forty under full way loaded with Japs, about three miles out from Santa Isabel. Attacking immediately before the Japs had a chance to disperse, many of the self-propelled barges flew into small pieces and capsized while those who escaped turned tail for the beach and safety.

That afternoon a second wave of *Enterprise* pilots went after the remaining barges. They found them on the mouth of a small river where the camouflage blended fairly well with the jungle-covered river. But not well enough. Again the Navy dive bombers went to work with bombs and machine guns. Only six of the barges ever reached Guadalcanal.

Following the destruction of these barges, the Japs launched a full-scale offensive to clean out the American forces, once and for all. It started with a terrific naval bombardment.

Barker, Fink, and Buell were prepared, as they had been spending their spare time digging a foxhole next to their bunks. They were all asleep when they heard the first Japs overhead. Then a big flare dropped right among them. They knew the flare would put the bug on them by giving the right position to the bombardment ships. Within seconds, the Japs opened up, pouring the shells into this area. Caldwell, Woodhull, Buell, Guillory, and Coolbaugh in the tent next theirs, rolled off and jumped and crawled in with the other four.

Coolbaugh who had the uppermost position in the dugout claimed it was an upper berth, but not soft. He counted the explosions from the ships and then counted them as they hit near by: "Now let's see, there were five explosions on the ships. There's still one left to go." The hits came some twenty-seven seconds after the guns flashed.

By the sound of the shells, the men knew how close they were and their size. A big shell caused the wind to blow through the palm trees. When the heavy rushing of air would sound like air going out of a tire it would be close, if not on you. Trees were cut off and fell over their hole. Twenty-five feet away two marines were shredded.

After it was over and they were alive, they stood and walked and felt the firm ground almost with reverence. They looked at Skipper Caldwell's tent—full of holes, a hole blasted through the bed he'd rolled out of, the tent post halved.

Again on the next night, about twelve, the pilots were awakened, but this time by artillery and rifle fire. The Japs had launched an all-out three-pronged land offensive against the slender Marine lines. The gunfire advanced to the southeast corner of Henderson Field itself near their planes.

But the Marines held.

Next morning when the pilots went down to their planes at daylight they found between fifty to sixty dead Japs left on the fighter field. Those Jap bodies had to be dragged or scraped up before the planes could take off. Japs had set up machine guns at the end of the take-off strip and as the first planes got under way they were shot at. The remaining planes kept below coconut treetop level when they took off while their rear-seat man shot at the machine gun positions. After these take-offs the Marines took over and wiped out the nests.

Next day, headquarters told Caldwell that had the Jap barge re-enforcements arrived it was quite possible that the Marines might not have held Henderson Field. The margin was that close.

These are but the fragments of the eleven *Enterprise* fliers' encounters in helping to break three invasion attempts on Guadalcanal. But in doing this, one after another they lost their planes, miraculously escaping with their lives.

Manford, for example, lost his plane when he skidded into a crater while taxiing at 60 miles per hour. Coolbaugh dropped his plane into a shell hole, repaired it with parts from other planes and flew it for a time, when it in turn became patching.

Fink was forced to make a water landing, out of gas, six miles off Guadalcanal.

Finally, a month after their arrival, relief came for the carrier pilots. Only one of the Big E planes was in commission. The pilots were half-sick, tired to death. And yet, when parting came, they left silently, half ashamed. They looked back upon the pocked, scarred field and thought of the fellow pilots they were leaving behind and of the odds against them.

23. Before Battle

It was the evening of October 25. The Big E was once more in Solomon waters. An enemy fleet had been sighted and a battle was expected in the morning. I decided to "tour" the *Enterprise* from Sky Control to Steering Room Aft and see what the spirit of a fighting ship was like on the eve of battle.

What I found is difficult to narrate. In comparison the highlights of battle, with planes zooming and falling and ships shooting, are easy to describe because they are thrilling and sensational. One records the deed. Much harder to depict convincingly are the long watches in which nothing happens except the strain of maintaining a condition of battle readiness at all times. The feeling of steaming deep into Jap-controlled waters, forever and ever expecting a night assault or a deadly torpedo to ram into your thin hull. The worry about such things as steam pipes which if hit will wipe out entire crews. Strain on the individual man who knows that on him rests the security of his ship and—with too few carriers left in the Pacific—perhaps the security of the Pacific. Or the personal fear of death, because on the ship are the torpedo warheads, bombs, incendiaries, ammunition, and powder—the very tools which are intended to wreak destruction upon the enemy.

Yet mixed with the tense alertness there were other feelings. When I heard John Crommelin speak to his pilots, there was the feeling of great leadership; when I saw men busily writing letters home just before the battle, there was the feeling of being close to loved ones; when I talked to John Hicks about books and poetry, he was talking about the things he was fighting for, the things he would want most if we came out of the battle—not material possessions and safety, but the free air of ideas to breathe and live in once more without fear.

The tense alertness this night struck me as incongruous. Night doesn't seem the time for vigil. Since the human animal quitted the jungle, night has meant rest and sleep and the restoration of tired muscles and the relaxation of nerves.

The pilots were gathered in the wardroom. Standing before them was Commander John G. Crommelin, Jr., the air officer, and he was talking. I thought: "This may be the beginning of a great battle."

It was a tense scene. Behind the pilots were the ship's officers not on watch. Fans were stirring. Their soft whirr turned the hot air, and if you got into the direct path it cooled the face—yet you sweated.

The pilots were nearly all under thirty, the majority about twenty-two and a few under twenty years. Yet their lean, taut faces showed that they were ripened men. Upon them would depend tomorrow's battle, if it were joined.

Looking upon the young fliers and watching them cup their wet faces into a damp inner sleeve, I realized how weak—in a sense—they were. Made of blood and flesh and bone and nerves. Soft, because flesh is so yielding to a shell fragment or an explosive bullet. Yet hard when you think of the long hours of flight day after day searching out the enemy. Many of these fellows had stretched their search this afternoon and had only a little gas left when they were snubbed up on the carrier deck. "Always narrow," I thought. "What keeps them going?"

Then I heard Commander John.

"You men do not need to be babied, and I don't intend to hold your hands. We know that the Jap task force we are looking for will have a three-to-one superiority over us. Four of our PBY patrols sighted the Jap task force. To give us the information we now have about the enemy, three of those four PBY crews were shot down: one got back." John let that sink in.

"They gave their best.

"You men will have the privilege tomorrow of proving the worth of your training, your schooling, our way of life as against the Japs'.

"The offensive strength we have in the Pacific at this moment is in the hands of you men in this room and of those on the *Hornet*.

"On you rests the safety of our Marines at Guadalcanal who have fought magnificently. Last night, they were bombarded again and the Japs made an assault upon their position but they held, proving their worth."

The large wardroom became small as one listened. In the corner of my eye, I noticed the mess boys standing in doorways listening to the eloquence of a fighting man.

"Wherever we have met the Jap at sea with our carriers, despite overwhelming odds, we have stopped them."

Commander John paused. Perhaps he was thinking of his young kid brother Richard who had been decorated with the Navy Cross for action at Coral Sea and Midway. Or of his other brothers. Henry, the second, was in destroyer command; Charlie was test-flying new Navy planes; Quentin was still in training. Five boys in the family and all of them Academy graduates. They were said to be all alike—aggressive fighters, opinionated and willing to fight at the drop of a hat. And wonderful friends because of their honesty and fearless convictions.

Commander John, or Uncle John as some of the pilots called him, came to the *Enterprise* after Midway. To the tired men who had fought for what seemed years he brought a new spirit. He was a ball of fire, full of enthusiasm. He breathed his hatred of the Jap and for what the Jap stood for.

He was out to kill as many Japs as he could and get the war over with.

To a man, the pilots who now listened to him respected John. They knew he was one of the best pilots in the Navy; some, who had seen him test fly at Anacostia, contended: "Commander John is the Navy's Number 1 pilot." For example, an English pilot once said in John's hearing that he had taken a new model plane out—one he had never seen before—and slow-rolled it on his first flight. Naturally, the next time John got to Barbers Point, Oahu, he made his first hop in the long-awaited fighter, the Hellcat, and as soon as he was 75 feet off the ground, put it into a beautiful slow roll.

"The Japs are determined to drive us out of the South Pacific. If they get through to Guadalcanal with their carriers tomorrow, the Japs will take it. If Guadalcanal falls, our lifeline to Australia will be menaced.

"To stop them, you must knock out their carrier force."

Having told them their responsibility, he assured them of their own skill. He told them they had been trained in the newest fighter and assault tactics by their able squadron leaders, Flatley, Coffin, and Lee. He told them that they had better planes which could take more punishment than any planes made. "Use them properly as you have been trained and you will shoot down the bastards in each encounter."

Finally, Commander John said: "And best of all, we are on the right side of this war. God is with us. Let's knock those Jap bastards off the face of the earth. God bless you . . ." In his mouth, the mixture of religion and profanity did not seem incongruous.

Most of the pilots went to their rooms. A few stopped to make toast and drink a cup of coffee.

I climbed the ladder up the island structure and went first to Sky Control, hoping to work my way down and then get a few hours' sleep before battle.

In Sky Control, one of the highest points of the ship, some 150 feet above the waterline, I found men huddled in groups in the dark. They were silent forms at first but after my eyes got adjusted to the blackness, I noticed that the night binoculars were constantly moving slowly over a certain wedge of water—each man's "piece of pie." I, too, studied the water and gradually saw the outline of ships. I counted them; it was not reassuring. There were so few in this task force and we were holding this vast front. I wondered, how can this small group of ships bend back the determined Jap?

We were steaming toward the enemy at 25 knots and better, leaving a white wake. Then the ships before us disappeared into the black gloom and in half a minute a squall was on us. It passed quickly. The stars were reflected on the wet forward end of our flight deck.

"Thought you knew better than to come up on a night like this, Gene," said Commander Livdahl, in command of the ship's gunnery. The silent hulks of the men seemed to agree. He moved a canvas-bottom chair beside him and offered it: "Glad you came. Sit down." And then together we fell silent with the motion of the ship and the low roar coming up the stacks from the engine room and you felt the concentration of men who are watching, alert.

A junior officer spoke up: "I wish someone would explain to me why in hell I don't get a letter from my wife. What's the matter with the mail? It's been two months. Damn it, can't they do that much for us? We've been away from our families two years now."

There's not much one can answer. Commander Livdahl said simply: "Two years is a long time. . . ."

Leaving the control tower and climbing down the steep, wet iron ladder carefully, I passed the bridge and found Admiral Kinkaid sitting on a long-legged chair studying the ocean. I knew that I would find him there again in the early morning before the sound of General Quarters. His Marine orderly was standing by. His flag secretary, Bob Taylor, said: "This is no time for a man with a quiet conscience to be up, Gene. Or have you lost the sense of time, living in this sealed ship?"

Admiral Kinkaid began pointing out some of the contrasts of carrier warfare as compared to World War I. He explained the complexity that airplanes had added. "Now a battle can be won or lost within five minutes. Trying to anticipate every eventuality keeps one awake," he added.

Navigator Ruble came out of his cabin to sight stars. "Come in and have a cup of coffee," he offered.

"No, thanks, I'm just looking the ship over before we go to battle. . . ."

"Just before the battle, mother . . ." a sailor hummed softly in the dark.

I went into the pilot house and saw the luminous glow of instruments. Shapes were outlined again. A command was given. A sailor repeated the command, adding "sir," and the ship took a new bearing. And again I marveled: A single man steers the ship, just as the sailor of old.

Beneath the pilot house were a dozen pair of eyes glued to night binoculars fixed upon the ocean. In their darkened room, day and night, these men study the water for the feathering wake of a periscope or the bubbly wake of a torpedo. Theirs is grueling work. But because of men like these and their shipmates, there was a feeling of security and confidence about the *Enterprise*.

As I unbolted the pilot house door, the room darkened behind me automatically, as it does when any aperture which might reveal light at sea is opened. I stepped outside and secured the door quickly. A sudden gust of cold air hit me and I realized how hot the innards of the ship were when it was dogged down. After all, we were in equatorial waters.

The ship seemed to draw up the heat of the day and then distill it at night. The skin of the ship sweat in rivulets.

On the flight deck planes were triced up, ready for the morning take-off. A mech was out, taking the air. He said: "Don't forget to write about the mechs who take care of these planes. We've been working more than eighteen hours each day. We're the guys that help them get there."

I thought: "Who on the ship doesn't help get them there?"

Forward, at Number 2 gun gallery, I found John Hicks. "What were you thinking about as I came along?" I asked. He was one of the officers who had heard John Crommelin talking to the pilots.

He took a deep breath. "It's the same thing, Gene. The longing for home. The New England hills. The woods. Talking with a girl. Books." It reminded me that I had not returned his volume of Robert Frost. "Better keep it until the battle's over," he said. Then he changed the subject abruptly. "By God, I have a lot of respect for the aviators. Those are the boys who are going to put a stop to this war."

I thought of the mech. "You have to get those pilots there so they can deliver the blow."

"That's too easy. What I'd like to do is to get right on the edge of things. I want to be one of the men who can honestly feel after this war is over: 'I was part of that small company which held the long thin Pacific front.' Isn't it amazing what a few men have held this Pacific? Not more than 500 pilots! It's even better than the battle of Britain."

"Those at home would consider you a part of that band, John. If you aren't, who is?"

"Perhaps they would," he answered. "But it's the way you feel about it yourself."

Below decks, I met Carpenter Reams. "Come along," he said, "I'm just getting ready to make my inspection." He is part of the repair crew on the Big E. It is his job and his men's

to prevent damage from getting out of hand during battle
and to control fires. For his splendid work on August 24, he
got a citation from Admiral Nimitz.

"Let's stop for sandwiches in the wardroom," I suggested.

"Make it the chief's quarters," he said. "Always better
sandwiches and coffee there. Chief petty officers are particu-
lar about their food." What Reams said is true. The chiefs
always eat best on any ship.

In the chief's room, Smith handed me a poem.

> We're out in the Pacific, patrolling,
> We've sighted nary a sail.
> If we're lucky, we'll get in in December
> For a two months' assortment of mail.
> We'll find out then what we're doing
> (The secrecy around us is dense).
> The papers will tell how we're striving
> For glory and national defense. . . .

There were several other verses telling about the food, the
strikes back home in war plants, and finished with this stanza:

> We've forgotten now what our home's like,
> And the fact that we once drove a car
> And still recall where our wives live,
> But we wish that they knew where we are.
> We remember still seeing our children,
> But they have forgotten us since.
> They think we are pictures that sit on a shelf,
> For glory and national defense.

In poems, letters, and conversation—even before battle—it
is always the same. The homesickness of the men. The longing for parents, wives, sweethearts, and children. I knew that
there was lonesomeness in many a home, too.

On the way back to my room I stopped to chat with an
enlisted man. Something seemed to be on his mind.

"It's this letter," he said, handing me a sheet. "I'd like you to read it. It's from my wife. I think it's the most wonderful letter in the world, but every time I read it I almost cry. I carry it around all the time."

I felt that I was intruding on something that was not meant for a second man's eyes, but he seemed very anxious that I read it. It said:

> Dear Jim: I pray for you always. When I'm in the 5 & 10¢ store, I stop and start praying. And when I'm waiting for a street car, I begin praying. And in theater lobbies, I pray. And when I'm cooking a meal, I pray God to keep you safe and bring you back, Jim. . . .

I pretended to read the rest. I mumbled how lucky I thought he was and went on to my room.

Of all the people I spoke to that night, Jim was the only one who was killed next day in the Battle of Santa Cruz.

24. *The Big E Takes It: Santa Cruz*

There are at least two ways to record a battle. One is under the aspect of eternity, so to speak—to make a reconstruction of all the accounts available, long after the event. The other, providing that one happened to be there, is to present a purely personal account of how it impinged on one's own senses and sensibilities. For what it is worth, I have elected to try the second method.

The Battle of Santa Cruz took place on October 26, in the waters off Santa Cruz Island in the Solomons group. The battle was another chapter in the history of the holding of the Solomons. In it the *Enterprise* was subjected to the heaviest attack any carrier has so far experienced in this war. These are excerpts from the notes I made during the battle:

4:20 A.M. Carpenter Reames wakes me. "Better get up, Gene, if you want to talk to the pilots." After I had shaved he came back: "So long, brother. Hope I see you tonight."

4:32 A.M. Little talk among the pilots in the wardroom. They look sleepy. They should; had a hard time flying the day before. Some planes made water landings due to their long search. You can stretch gas just so far. "Better eat a big one," says Jimmy Daniels. "Can't tell when or where you'll have your next meal." Birney Strong looks over. "Hey, writer, do you want to ride with me?" Young Sablan, the mess steward, is slow in bringing my hotcakes. Poor kid, he was working past midnight. When do they sleep? On a blackboard against the wall are figures and notes written by John Crommelin during his talk to the pilots last night. They remind us that we are outnumbered two-and-a-half to one in the enemy's own waters. Someone has chalked up over the figures: "BIG E *vs.* JAPAN."

4:58 A.M. Chaplain Young comes in to the ready room and slips into the seat next to me. "Thought maybe I could help," he says simply. I think of yesterday's church service. Young talked of Christ sleeping in a boat on the Sea of Galilee and when the waves frightened the disciples they woke Him and He asked: "Why are ye afraid?"

5:06 A.M. Up on the bridge, it's dark as midnight. The first search planes are on deck. Commander Spud Monohan, assistant air officer, at the mike, has a swell voice which booms over the loudspeaker: "Stand clear of propellers. Start engines." You expect a simultaneous roar, but instead there is a winding noise, then individual engines cough. The roar gradually increases. The exhaust flames come out a clear, incredibly clean blue. Will Jap subs see the flames?

Dawn is streaking in. For the first time I know where the east is.

Admiral Kinkaid is wearing the same torn shirt he had on

yesterday. Maybe slept in it. Notice his shoes are highly shined though. Odd the irrelevant details that strike you at times like these.

More than the normal green in the sky. The sea is calm. The sun really jumps out of the horizon. Light, fluffy, gold-tinted clouds. Flying fish zoom low over the water like miniature torpedo planes—perish the thought!

Search planes lift off the deck easily, each with a 500-pound bomb. The noise is gone.

Admiral Kinkaid tells me: "A PBY made contact this morning. Looks like a fight. Need more pilots like him."

Couldn't be on a better ship for the fight. I watch Commander Ruble, the ship's navigator, take sights on the barely risen sun. They don't come steadier than Ruble. Plays good poker, too.

"Waiting for contact reports adds years," says the admiral.

I climb to Sky Control to get a steel helmet. After seeing experienced crew members tuck trouser legs into socks, I follow their example. This is to prevent flash burns. Many of the deaths in naval battles are due to burns.

The ship is tense. It seems to tighten up in front of your eyes. Orderly runs up and hands message to Kinkaid, who doubles his fist. "We've got them! Here's a report on a battleship contact." Admiral adds, "Good bait, but not our target. We must wait for more developments."

An officer in the flight control office says, "We ought to send out our attack force now. Those Jap carriers will be sitting behind the battleships. Why in hell do we wait?"

I return to signal bridge and nod to Lieutenant Shannan. That bird has a grin all the time; it fits naturally.

Squadron Commander Bucky Lee sends in contact report on carriers. The tenseness lets up as we know the enemy is found. Suddenly planes are emitted from the *Enterprise*.

8:12 A.M. An hour later, and still nothing develops on the

contact. What a war! You don't get to see a Jap, much less his ship.

Loudspeaker system announces that Lieutenant Strong and his wingman Irvine got two hits on the Jap carrier *Shokaku!* (That's one of Japan's biggest and best.) Bert Harden says: "Must be a story there, Gene. They were on the other side of the searching parties. They must have flown 160 miles to make contact. Wonder if they'll have enough gas to make it back?"

9:40 A.M. "Put on flashproof clothing," says the loudspeaker. "Scouts intercepted a Jap force about 60 miles out."

9:45 A.M. Enter rain squall. Maybe the Japs won't find us.

10:11 A.M. AA fire seen from *Hornet* about 10 miles off. Clean blue sky sooted with AA. Bursts are black roses opening slowly.

The *Hornet* is hit! Flame flashes high forward near signal bridge. I see her plainly with a telescope. There are flaming streaks in sky, as planes are shot down. I hope none of them are ours. The *Hornet* smoking badly and a high plume is going into the sky.

10:25 A.M. Can't see any enemy airplanes. The sea is calm and the *Hornet* is still smoking. (My co-worker, AP Correspondent McMurtry, was on the *Hornet* signal bridge, which I did not know at the time. His hands and face were badly burned.)

11:13 A.M. *Here come the Japs!* Our AA and 5-inchers drown out everything, but not your fear. I flatten out on the steel deck. God, I'm scared. Admiral Kinkaid is the only man up.

Japs are rocking out of the sky like apples. The ship is gyrating, twisting and bending to avoid. I get up to see the attack. My pencil breaks and Shannan gives me his. For the first time I'm uncontrollably angry at the Japs. Maybe it is because I am so damn scared. The ship rocks as if from an earthquake. We're hit!

I watch a plane waddle 30 feet over the side with the heavy shakes. We must be hit hard. Smoke rolls out of the deck.

Near misses are falling all around us. A column of water is higher than the signal bridge. Tons of water. No one dead on deck so far as I can see. Was there an explosion below?

11:27 A.M. Loudspeaker: "Periscope of submarine sighted off starboard bow."

11:33 A.M. Enemy dive bombers reported coming in.

11:42 A.M. Loudspeaker again: "All fires have been put out." Must have done a magnificent job.

11:48 A.M. *Here come the Japs again!* The ship ducks into small squalls. Bet Gunnery Officer Livdahl is cussing. This rain squall business is not to the liking of his gunners.

This attack I decide to watch standing up. Not so scaring. Like hell! I'm down and scared. Kinkaid is lighting one cigarette from another. I get up. The *Enterprise* AA fire is accurate. I see Jap planes explode. It's impossible to suppress a sense of triumph and satisfaction and gratitude towards our gunners and fighters.

I see five burning Jap planes in the sky at one time. They fall before I can count up to four. When they hit water, gas and oil burn in a flaming circle for a minute. Good gravestones for Japs.

Admiral says: "Burns, you're the most favored civilian alive. You're seeing the greatest carrier duel of history. Perhaps it will never happen again."

See bubbly torpedo wakes passing ship. They must travel 40 miles an hour. No, forgot to allow for ship's speed.

See the destroyer *Porter* 200 yards off stop to pick up one of our aviators who landed in water. Loudspeaker: "Cease firing! Cease firing! Our own planes." (One of our pilots, taking his life in his hands, is making a dive upon a torpedo which is circling in the water. Apparently spotted it from high up, took the chance of being shot down for a Jap and strafed it to set it off or call attention to it.)

The *Porter* frantically tries to get under way to avoid the torpedo. It doesn't. There's a fountain just as the torpedo hits. Then a tremendous puff of smoke, like a railway engine blowing off a smoke cloud. I can't believe that I saw the whole thing with my own eyes. One doesn't see these things except in newsreels.

Jap pilots return to attack. They are more respectful. They drop bombs 500 yards away.

New battleship is hit. Some smoke. No other explosion. What would she do if all the planes aimed at us were turned on her?

I see AA from rear-seat guns of parked planes on *Enterprise* deck.

The ship shakes. Perhaps we're hit again. It shakes once more. Near misses seem to rock our ship most.

Loudspeaker: "Enemy sub on starboard, amidships." Wonder what men below decks think.

Within thirty seconds, the loudspeaker comes back: "Belay that. Porpoises, not a submarine contact." Everyone laughs with nervous relief.

Suddenly a flaming Jap plane crashes into the destroyer U.S.S. *Smith*, about 150 feet off port side. Tremendous fires burn higher than ship. Her after guns keep firing. "Damn nice seamanship," says the admiral, watching her maneuvers.

A 500-pound bomb slants over our signal bridge. A tall first baseman could have speared that one. Explosion alongside. A column of water falls on ship and puts out a gasoline fire. God's with us.

The *Smith's* guns are still throwing up a barrage. She's keeping her place in the screen although her whole front is enveloped in flames. The battleship fire is out.

The Japs are leaving. That is, there seems to be no more around. Doubt if many "left" us. Most of them seemed to fall into the water. This attack lasted about four minutes. Ships prepare a lifetime for a battle which lasts a few minutes.

The destroyer *Smith* is plowing her bow under our wake to put out her fire. Smart cooky, that skipper.

I see some of our planes returning to land. Back on deck, I notice some strange pilots. Must be from the *Hornet*. One's wounded. (I learned later it was Lieutenant Benny Moore of the *Hornet*.)

12:15 P.M. Our scouts report enemy torpedo planes approaching! Those Japs don't give us a chance to cool our guns.

12:22 P.M. Watch planes trying to come in. They're scared this time. We got almost all of them. None of them are able to come into our screen. This ship will ride out the war with this crew.

12:30 P.M. The attack is over! (The last five Jap torpedo planes were shot down. Of the eighty-odd planes which attacked, they were the last five of thirty-two shot down. Not a bad hour's work!)

I went below. Many planes were burned on hangar deck. I saw horribly burned faces.

Off the wardroom, forward in the officers' country, a bomb had exploded. My room was no more; I lost everything, but it hardly seemed to matter. There was a mixed smell of rags and flesh and Foamite. I saw a man's whole liver as the ship heeled over and it slipped on the oily floor. The men worked silently. "About sixty killed here forward," said someone in response to my question.

Carpenter Reames came past. He shook hands. "God, I'm glad we're both alive," he said and went on with his work.

Back on deck I learned that Ensign Marshall Field, Jr., was hurt. Two days before I had told him: "Marshall, don't go

and be a hero because the AP will have to use the story."
(His father's paper, the Chicago *Sun*, was suing the Associated Press.)

Gunnery Officer Lidhval told me of a little Mexican shell-
man from Los Angeles named Cordoba. As he moved shells
from shell locker to fuse box, he kissed them. When he had
time, he shook his fist at the Japs.

If I heard it once, I heard it a thousand times: "Well, Gene,
I guess you got yourself something to write about this time,
eh?"

Bert Harden told me: "The Japs used at least 175 planes.
More than eighty-four attacked us. Our gunners shot down
about thirty-four and our fighters got more. I doubt if the
Japs got ten of their planes back." (We lost twenty-three
planes; nine pilots and four rear-seatmen were lost, a later
tabulation showed.)

Lieutenant Art Kelly of the air office thought we may have
gotten one Jap carrier, damaged another, damaged one battleship, a heavy Jap cruiser, a light cruiser, and 160 planes. The
Japs got the *Hornet* and the *Porter*, damaged the *Smith* and
got three bad hits on the Big E (they were partially repaired
within four days) and a hit on a battleship.

25. "*All That I Could Ask For*"

Sitting mile high over the *Enterprise*, on the lookout for
Jap planes, Pilot Albert David Pollock saw far below the
bubbly wake of a Jap torpedo running in circles between the
carrier and the *Porter* which was coming to a stop in order
to pick up a plane crew.

Dave thought fast. There was a chance of strafing the running torpedo and setting off or jamming its delicate mech-

anism. More important, by strafing he would attract the *Porter's* attention in time to escape its mortal danger.

Looking at the gun fire from our ships and the falling Jap planes, Dave knew that he had little chance of getting out with a whole skin. However, he shoved into a dive. As expected, the ships in the formation opened up on him and the tracers streaked into his plane. But still he came on. Gunners finally saw that it was one of our planes and held their fire.

Dave made three passes on the circling torpedo, churning the water with his guns. The *Porter* saw him, understood his signal at once and got under way. But it was a fraction of a minute too late. The torpedo hit amidships and the destroyer had to be abandoned and sunk. (Pollock finished his day by nailing down a Jap dive bomber and a Jap torpedo plane.)

The crew for which the *Porter* had stopped were Lieutenant Batten and Gunner Holmgrin. "On the way out to make the attack on the Japs, we were the last plane in a formation of nine," said Batten. "Japs jumped us out of the sun about 70 miles out and about a dozen made passes at us.

"We let the leader have several bursts at 400 yards and he dropped. Then the next one popped right up and Holmgrin picked him off and he blew into little pieces just aft of us. One of those pieces hit my elevator and knocked a big hole in it. As a result I lost elevator control and then a cloudful of Japs dropped down out of the sun at us."

Rex Holmgrin finished the story. "Tracers were pouring out of all of them. After one of them made a run at us a hole appeared in our wing and then it began burning badly. I hollered to my pilot: 'Mr. Batten, our wing is afire!' He looked and said: 'I'll say it is. I'll try to set the plane into the water.'

"Mr. Batten put it into a steep dive through a heavy cloud. Coming out, he said: 'Rex, I think the fire's burning out.' Soon only a little smoke came from the wing.

"Then he said: 'I think we can make it back all right now. No use losing our ship.'

"Mr. Batten climbed and then one of the ailerons broke off and all of our lateral control was gone. The only thing which kept us from spinning," Holmgrin explained, "was a rudder which, too, was damn near shot away. But as we flew in closer we spotted our own formation. The battle was in full tilt so we stayed about 20 miles out watching it.

"We had the satisfying privilege of seeing four Jap planes come out and hit the water. They don't bounce," said Holmgrin. "We checked our parachutes, and strapped ourselves in for the blow. This was going to be no rocking chair landing with nothing to slow us up, one wheel down, the elevators shot away, no control, a burned wing and a ton torpedo still fastened to our belly. But Mr. Batten could fly a washtub if you put wings on it.

"He brought her down as pretty as a Catalina, but he whacked his head against the control board and it knocked him out bloody and cold. However, he came to and managed to make it out to the wing while I launched the life raft and within a few minutes I was able to tell him: 'Here comes a destroyer to pick us up.'

"I had no more than said that when an explosion knocked us out of our raft into the water. We didn't know that the destroyer coming for us had been torpedoed.

"We got back in our raft and paddled over to the *Porter* and were hoisted aboard. We found everyone quietly attending their duties, preparing to abandon ship. There was no confusion—not a peep even out of the injured. An officer, in fact, came to us and said: 'I'm sorry, we're pretty busy right now. Please make out the best you can for a little bit.'

"Men brought us cigarettes and as we smoked one of our destroyers dropped depth charges for the Jap sub which had injured the *Porter*. Ashcans produced two oil slicks and brought up debris. Then a second destroyer came alongside and took off the crew while bombs from the third Jap attack dropped all around us."

The rescue ship was the *Shaw*, back in action after having had her bow blown off at Pearl Harbor.

With the *Hornet* burning and the *Porter* exploding, the destroyer *Smith* was aflame from the torched Jap dive bomber which had plummeted down and crashed into her forward deck, about 100 yards away from the *Enterprise*.

Admiral Kinkaid later signaled this message to her:

"THE MAGNIFICENT PERFORMANCE OF THE SMITH IN ACTION GAVE A THRILL OF ADMIRATION TO EVERYONE WHO SAW IT. WITH FORECASTLE AFLAME THE GALLANT SHIP MAINTAINED STATION IN THE SCREEN AND CONTINUED TO GIVE PROTECTION TO THE CARRIER AGAINST ATTACKING ENEMY PLANES. WELL DONE."

After the attack, I boarded the *Smith* while survivors were picking up twisted fragments of the Jap plane.

Lieutenant Commander Hunter Wood, Jr., the captain, told me that a torpedo explosion scattered fragments and flames even into the Number 1 engine room; then two of the *Smith's* ready ammunition rooms holding 5-inch shells exploded and this was followed with a series of minor explosions.

The skipper and his junior officers and the enlisted men all spoke of Ensign Neal Scott. The captain told me that he had come aboard the *Smith* on October 10, just 16 days before this action. "He told me," said Commander Wood, "that he had joined the Navy for action. They had made him a paymaster and he did not want 'to fight the war from dry land.' So I gave him the Number 2 turret. He caught on quick and the crew liked him."

While talking, Commander Wood picked his way over the

debris to the fire-wrenched Number 2 turret, now twisted into junk.

"This is the gun," he said. "He must have been standing here." He took a position beside a hole where the Jap plane buried itself into the deck.

"Scott was badly burned. His eyes were gone."

"As they carried him aft, Scott heard the voice of Lieutenant Zimmerman, in charge of the guns, and shouted: '*Keep those guns firing, boys.*'"

Commander Wood called upon members of his crew to tell how the *Smith* fought her raging fires and kept on shooting. Modestly the men revealed the story. Three threw burning ammunition overboard. Others rigged hoses to fight the fire. Others freed trapped men. Some flooded burning compartments. A torpedo-man fought through flames to jettison the *Smith's* forward torpedoes. Every act courted death.

They all ended up by saying: "Lieutenant Zimmerman kept the guns firing."

Zimmerman disclaimed this. "It was my crew. They just kept kicking out the shells until the last Jap plane was gone. We think we helped shoot down seven during the entire action.

"While our ship was fighting the fire," he added, "my men jerked out the hot gun barrels with their naked hands and dipped them into the water to cool them. The water sizzled and boiled. Two with the meat burned out of their palms I ordered to sick bay, but they sneaked out and got into the ammunition line to pass the 53-pound shells."

The ship's doctor, Lieutenant Aloysius J. Havlik, added: "Yes, and all the other wounded men I had down below wanted to go up and keep on fighting, even Scotty."

"Who was the last man to talk to Scotty?" I asked.

"Svart, the pharmacist's mate," the doctor said. "I'll send for him."

When Svart came I asked: "What were Scott's last words?"

"Well, it wasn't exactly talking. He spelled out a message for me to give to his folks. He did it carefully letter by letter so that I would get it straight."

He searched three pockets, pulled it out and handed it to me.

It read:

"DR. L. R. SCOTT, GOLDSBORO, NORTH CAROLINA. TO HAVE YOU AND MOTHER FOR THESE TWENTY-FOUR YEARS HAS BEEN ALL THAT I COULD ASK FOR IN THIS WORLD. NEAL."

26. Men Make the Ship

As soon as the first Jap dive bomber scored his hit on the *Enterprise* at 11:25 A.M., Chief Shipfitter Joseph J. Forrest fought his way through steel rubble, dense smoke, and a maze of wiring from damaged electric circuits to extinguish the fires in the vicinity of high octane gas pumps. Below were ammunition magazines.

"I had to work fast to put out the fires. There was at least 10 feet of water to be pumped out before we could open the compartment hatch, under which several men were trapped. We had to fight through smoke and rubbage. But we got them out by 5:30 that night."

In that handling room, waiting for the compartment door to be opened, was Vincente Sablan, an officers' mess attendant, a native of Guam. At 11 A.M., when Jap planes were reported, the little fellow had his ear phones on, ready to relay information of any damage to his compartment.

Then the bomb hit and exploded. Sablan said: "I thought the whole ship was falling in on us. Long after the explosion things kept falling. Water poured down from the hatch and heavy smoke came with it. I thought maybe the Japs were using gas. All of the lights were out and it was pitch black and smoky and the water kept seeping in, inch by inch, until it was waist deep. And then it came to here," he said, leveling off his hands at his shoulder sockets. "I stood on my toes, afraid."

However the little mess boy kept his telephone communications going, not once failing to report accurately to the damage control department.

"Oh, yes, sir," said Sablan, "I was scared perpetual for six hours. When I got to thinking about the air my heart started beating faster and I prayed hard, first in English and then my mother's prayers to St. Joseph and Santa Antonia, and then when things got real bad, I talked direct to God."

Negro Mess Attendant William Pinckney's battle station was in the 5-inch ammunition handling room. It was not until three days later, when Gunner James R. Bagwell told how his life was saved, that Pinckney's story came to light.

Pinckney's very modest account was as follows: "When the attack on the *Enterprise* started, I shut off the ventilators like I was asked to by the captain, and sent the ammunition up and passed the word that we were standing by for an attack. Then a 5-inch shell went off on the port side and I was knocked out.

"I must have been laid up for about five minutes before I really came to strong enough to do something. Fires were burning hot and the smoke was real heavy and I felt some guy under me. Finally one guy got up and yelled: 'Whereabouts is the God-darn door?' and I said: 'I sure don't know.' I got up and felt around where I imagined it ought to be and then I saw a little light coming from overhead. I climbed up and saw a large fire burning all around so I came on back down.

"About this time, I felt a little boiling water trickling down

and I said: 'Well, Mr. Pinckney, the Japs got you this time
sure.' But I started up when this other guy comes along. No,
can't say as I recollect the guy's name. He was taller'n me
and he reached up and fell back and asked: 'How's for
helpin'?' I started to grab hold of a piece of iron to shin up
and it was shorted so I got me an electric shock which upset
me and I fell down.

" 'Mr. Pinckney, you just got to make it,' I said to myself,
so I got mad and grabbed hold of a piece of pipe and climbed
and was safe."

I went to Gunner Bagwell, whose name Pinckney didn't
"recollect," to learn how the Negro, although badly burned,
saved his life.

Bagwell said: "I tried to get out of the ammunition handling room which was burning fiercely and full of smoke.
I tried to climb out but I burned my hands and fell back and
went unconscious. The next think I knew, Pinckney was
trying to hoist me up but he dropped me because he received
an electric shock.

"Then I passed out again and came to with that colored
boy dragging me to safety on the hangar deck. The skin was
burned off his hands, his right leg and his back. God only
knows how he handled me because I weigh twenty pounds
more than him."

When Pinckney was confronted with this evidence, he
said: "Well, I did help a little here and there. The guy was
pretty heavy but he didn't seem so when I got my mind made
up. After I got him to the hangar deck, he seemed to be sur-
viving pretty good so I left him."

Commander Boone, the Exec, added another fact a week
later: "After Pinckney brought Bagwell up, he went below
again to help others."

And sure enough, asked about it, Pinckney admitted: "Yeh,
I guess that's right. When this first guy seemed to be sur-

viving pretty good, I went down below to see if I could help someone else but they were all dead and killed and I couldn't help anyone."

One of the day's hits was a freak. The heavy armor-piercing bomb slanted through the flight deck, passed out of the hull near the waterline and then exploded outside of the ship, hurling fragments back into the carrier.

Ensign Marshall Field, Jr., of Chicago, directing the fire of a forward gun, related how he was looking up and saw the bomb above his mount. "We caught the plane in our fire about halfway down its dive, when it was released. I looked up and saw the bomb about 100 feet right above me.

"As the bomb hit a short distance behind us, I could hear the splintering, cracking noise like firewood snapping. Then there was a terrific explosion and a flash. I felt myself picked off my feet and hurtling through space. Then I lit on my back on the fo'c'sle. When I got up I was bleeding."

Warren Lee, the fire control man, added: "Mr. Field was ordered to go to the captain's country which was used for a first-aid station. But by then things were getting hot again and the word was passed: 'Stand by for torpedo planes and dive bombers,' so Field got into the mount again and helped pick out targets.

"Yes, sir," young Lee said: "I was wounded, too, in the leg, but our gun helped shoot down seven planes."

Looking at the gun mount where the young multi-millionaire and the seaman first class were huddled, I couldn't help thinking it was a miracle that they were alive. The heavy boiler plate mount was riddled with holes.

Only 3 per cent of a ship's company at most see action from topside and watch Jap planes drop into the water. Six decks down they hear the word: "Prepare for dive bombers."

They put on hot flashproof clothing and steel helmets and stand by. Deep in the ship a near miss often feels worse than a hit. The ship rides like a roller-coaster as the explosion whips its sides. Loose gear is hurled through compartments.

"Down here we know that there's a job to be done," said Lieutenant Commander Yost, after the Santa Cruz battle. "All you'd have to do is to see how our American boys are under fire to know that they're made of mighty fine stuff. Here, talk to them."

I asked Jack H. McVey, twenty, fireman first class, how long he had been in the Navy.

"Three years, sir. My battle station is engine room communications. The day of the attack, I was on steady for sixteen hours and then I had a four-hour watch later. I have something to do all the time so it doesn't bother me."

"I helped put the *Enterprise* in commission," said Steward M. Steele, twenty-four, machinist's mate first class. "I figure that this ship will tie up alongside the dock in Pearl Harbor when this war is over."

A fellow standing near by spoke up: "That guy doesn't know when to be worried. He was singing 'Deep in the Heart of Texas' while the bombs were exploding kind of like the handclaps that are supposed to go with it. I'll bet it's the first time it was ever sung like that!"

Watertender Second Class Harold Bace said: "I was pretty shaky. The ship felt like a rowboat with those near misses. But I kept my fires up and kept my eye on everything. What helps is that you think ahead trying to find an answer to every question. As for my six men, they handled their jobs perfectly."

When the last attack group had left the *Enterprise* three scout bombing planes were left on board. At once the pilots—Estes, Ritchie, and Erwin—volunteered to fly them into the enemy. The planes were loaded with deadly 1,000-pounders and launched.

Estes reported the action: "As we proceeded to the scene of the attack, we sighted two *Kongo* type battleships, cruisers and cans. Our gas was getting low so we elected to concentrate our three-man attack on one of the battleships. We gained 12,000 feet. Riding down a cumulus cloud gave us protection and we caught the Japs flat-footed.

"Erwin's bomb was a near miss off the bow but the bomb spout must have washed some of the Japs overboard, I hope. Ritchie hit Number 2 turret and must have wiped out some of the gun crews, while mine hit amidships a little on the starboard side."

The anti-aircraft from this concentration of Jap ships must have been pretty terrific, so I asked him about it.

"Yes, there was quite a bit of AA fire." He grinned. "As we scrammed out, low to the water, the Japs even fired their main batteries into the water ahead of us."

"And Zeros?"

"Yeh, they came down too, but our rear-seat boys kind of discouraged them. But the best sight of all was the fire we started on that battleship. There must have been some powder explosions because the column of smoke was miles high even when we were only a short distance from the action."

Cool as any exploit of the day was that turned in by Signal Officer Lieutenant Robin Lindsey of San Francisco.

The morning of October 26, Robin and Jimmy Daniels, his understudy, were on the landing platform when the Jap bombers, polished and shiny, arrived. Right off, both men were knocked down by the water spout from a near miss. They got up and were knocked down again by the concussion of near-by 5-inch guns.

When the first wave of Jap bombers were over, there was

a few minutes' pause and Robin saw his chance to land some of the *Enterprise* planes returning from their long morning search. By now, he knew, some of these planes must be flying on their imagination and each time they circled might be the last. So, while the ship was heeling to port and then to starboard at 25 degree angles, Lindsey brought in ten planes.

After the tenth landed, the Jap torpedo plane attack started. As torpedoes streaked by the ship, both Jimmy and Robin jumped into planes triced to the deck and manned rear-seat guns. Their wish was granted. A torpedo plane came in from astern and made the very fatal mistake of turning his belly toward the two signal officers. The men plowed their .30-caliber tracers into the plane and plunged it into the sea.

"It was the most fun I've ever had," commented Daniels.

Over half of Lieutenant Stanley "Swede" Vejtasa's ammunition was shot away during the first attack at Santa Cruz in downing two enemy dive bombers and a possible third. Then he saw a flight of eleven Jap torpedo planes making for the Big E. He dived on their rear, shot down five and caused three more to jettison their torpedoes before his ammunition gave out; two other boys in his flight polished off the remaining three.

If those of us on the carrier who counted eighty-four planes in four waves did not know of this possible fifth attack, it was due to Swede.

Lieutenant Commander James H. Flatley, who commanded Fighting Squadron Ten, said: "Swede's act of destroying seven planes and a possible eighth during a single engagement is the outstanding single combat air engagement of this war to date." He added: "His individual act may have saved the *Enterprise*."

Lieutenant Stanley Vejtasa, of Circle, Montana, is modest. He gave credit to others: "I knew I had three good fliers protecting my rear, so I just helped myself to an extra platter of Japs."

As division leader, Swede took off with Lieutenant Leroy Harris, his wingman, Lieutenant Stanley Erdman Ruehlow, and Ensign William Leder. "We climbed like cats shinnying up flagpoles," he said, "and saw six Jap dive bombers pour out of the 10 o'clock sun.

"There were those six fat babies," Swede went on. "Five above and one below. Of course, that sixth one was a helping of white turkey and we shot him down."

"That one was yours, Swede," Leder said indignantly. "The five Japs got into the carrier but we caught two of them pulling away from their dive. Ruehlow got one and the other one goes for the flight. A third left a streak of smoke as he got away from us."

This time lanky Harris shoved up his big hands. "Cut out that 'for the flight' stuff. Those were your ducks."

Swede grinned. "We climbed back up to 10,000 feet and were just cruising comfortable, when we spotted the eleven torpedo planes. Tex Harris got one and I got one. Both those Japs torched off. "The remaining nine Japs plunged into a cloud but we followed them right in. I got behind a group of three."

Ruehlow interrupted. "Where do you get that 'we' business, Swede?"

Unruffled, Swede continued: "We stuck right on their tails and salted those birds down with .50-caliber rocksalt."

He got into his story now, demonstrating with outspread hands. "I eased up right behind him and I got me three. It was like shaking down apples. Then I saw another and rolled up and tackled him. He dropped his fish and tried to sneak for cover. Then I followed another Jap chap as he went past. He dropped his freight in the open sea. About the same time two others scattered.

"I was out of ammunition but they were easy to scare, so I closed in on the remainder and they scattered like chickens with a hawk coming in. "Just think, if I'd only had more ammunition!"

He claimed only partial credit for his extraordinary achievement. "I knew my three men were protecting my rear, just like Skipper Flatley had worked out with us. But why in hell don't you talk with the Skipper?" Swede added. "He broke his foot two days before the battle, went up against doctor's orders, tangled with two Jap battleships of the *Kongo* class and strafed them to divert their AA fire, thereby making it easier for our torpedo bombers to slip a fish into them. That's what I call a real job of flying."

During the second attack by dive bombers, one of the ship's radio antennae was knocked out of commission. Lieutenant Dwight M. Williams, radio officer, immediately went aloft to the foretop, the highest point of the ship, to effect repairs. At the precise moment Williams restored the antenna casualty, the third attack wave of Jap dive bombers arrived over the ship and commenced "peeling off."

"As the first dive bomber attempted to pull out of his dive," said Williams, "it virtually disintegrated before my eyes. Lieutenant Commander Benny Mott, directing our ack-ack over the bull-horn, was doing a terrific job. However, the Jap had carried out his mission before he was killed—he had released his bomb.

"I've often heard of men who, with death imminent, relive their lives within an inordinately brief interval. Something tantamount to that happened to me as I watched that small sphere increase in size while it plummeted directly toward me! Those who have been bombed know that if it appears as a ball—that is, you can't see its length—then it definitely has your name on it! It's amazing how many thoughts crowd through your mind at such a moment. Mine went something like this:

"This is it! Guess my Quaker School teacher wasn't wrong when she said, 'If thee follows thy father's footsteps, by entering the military service, thee shall probably die a violent death!' That damned Hindu fortune-teller in Bombay certainly knew her stuff when she predicted that I'd live till my hair turned white. It's probably turning white this instant! Am willing to bet a thousand yen that the case of that damned bomb is made of scrap-metal we used to sell to the bastards! Why the hell don't we turn? Wonder how many others beside me will get it due to this one? What an inane, impossible way to slip my cable! Goddam isolationists responsible for this bloody mess: 'We mustn't fortify Guam; it would cause a breach in our diplomatic relations with Japan!' Goddam it, why don't we turn? Guess this egg will go right through the foretop and probably let go on the bridge. That means the Old man, that war correspondent, and the signal force—nice messy job for the first lieutenant's gang. Why the bloody hell don't we TURN! Surely hope that it's an 'A.P.' and not a bloody 'daisy-cutter!' Why the hell couldn't I have had just one date with that femme, one chance to see my Scottie Duffer? Hot damn, it's getting longer! Christ! what a turn! O.K., you bastards, missed me again! One time you Samurai bums can't yell banzai!!"

27. Birney Strong Gets a Carrier

Lieutenant Birney Strong had a resolve which was stronger, perhaps, than that of any of the other scouting pilots vectored out that morning to search for the enemy carriers. He was going to do more than find the carrier. He was going to "get" it—for good, personal reasons.

Strong, a Naval Academy man, went into the war with 800 carrier hours and now, in October, he had more than 1,400 hours—almost every hour dangerous. In February he had bombed Makin in the Gilbert Islands off the *Yorktown*. In March he had bombed transports at Lae and Salamaua. He had pushed his heavy Douglas torpedo plane, with a 1,950-pound torpedo, over the 7,000-foot Owen Stanley range, New Guinea, to catch the Japs by surprise. He had raided Tulagi in May, where his squadron found twelve ships "and it just naturally was impossible not to get a hit." In the Coral Sea battle—the first carrier duel of history—he scored a hit on a Jap carrier.

He'd no more than returned to Pearl Harbor from that deal when the Midway battle loomed. He went again, leaving behind the girl who had promised to marry him. His carrier didn't get in on the battle and he came back to Honolulu and was married. After five weeks with Scouting Five, he came aboard the *Enterprise*.

In the August 24 battle Lieutenant Strong located one of the Jap carriers but was driven off by Zeros and AA and returned to find his own carrier hurt and smoking. His first reaction was anger; then, remorse: "Why didn't I push home my attack on the carrier when I had the chance?" Before he landed, almost out of gas, he resolved: "I'll smack the next Jap carrier, sure as hell."

Revenge filled his thoughts day and night and he couldn't crowd them out of his mind. The *Enterprise*, wounded, returned to Pearl Harbor. Strong told his bride: "I have to go back to hit a Jap carrier before I can come home with a clear mind."

When the *Enterprise* took on her new air group, Strong went to Air Officer Crommelin and begged for the chance to go out with them and hit a Jap carrier while there were still some left.

Crommelin debated. The kid had flown more combat hours off carriers than any other pilot. Could he take the strain? Was this a temporary whim? Strong's intensity convinced Crommelin and he took the boy with him.

As dawn broke October 26, Strong and his wingman, Skinhead Irvine, were well away from the carrier. They flew on and nothing developed. Others on these patrols had likewise sighted nothing. "Queer," he thought; "maybe the Japs are scared this time." But his eyes kept searching. It seemed as though it was always at the end of the "leg" of the flight that contact developed.

Then came the report he was waiting for. Lieutenant David W. Welch and his wingman, Lieutenant (j.g.) Bruce A. McGraw, had found a Jap battleship force. Strong's decision was instantaneous. He had finished his search. He motioned to Irvine and curved his plane into an interception course. He calculated his position and checked his fuel supply.

Irvine and Strong had flown 100 miles on this interception course when they heard their scouting commander, "Bucky" Lee, report a contact with two Jap carriers. Strong studied his gas gauge again; it was low. But this was the chance he had been praying for, the kind of chance that comes once in a lifetime. Again he plotted his course and once more curved his plane for the new junction. It was an added 80 miles away—long, gas-consuming miles.

Nursing his gas, Strong climbed gradually as he and his wingman flew into position. He knew their only chance was to come in high, down-sun and down-wind, and maybe catch the Japs by surprise. Then, there on the horizon and growing larger, was a sight even better than the one which had possessed him for months—two large carriers, the best Japan had.

"It's a funny thing," he said later. "I wasn't a bit scared.

I'd gone out with the *Enterprise* because I wanted just such a crack at them. I wanted to prove to my air officer I could do it. I remembered the time I came back and found my ship wounded. I figured that I could get that Jap if I had to fly into him."

Gradually getting bigger was the prettiest sight a Jap-killing pilot can ever hope to see—acres of pine-yellow decks.

Strong wondered how Bucky Lee had penetrated the enemy's air and surface screens to develop such a beautiful and accurate contact report. He wondered whether Lee and his wingman had made it back.

As he flew into position, Strong knew that their puny two-man attack would certainly provoke a terrific concentrated AA barrage, and that their slow planes would certainly rouse a cloud of enemy fighters. Chances of escaping were slim; their fuel was so low that return to the Big E was almost certainly prevented. Evasive tactics would drain what remained doubly fast. These things Strong had against him; but against his revenge they did not count.

It was a beautiful morning, the waves below them were flecked with white. As far as the eye could see the ceiling stretched, with scattered cumulus puffing up like gobs of meringue.

Again Strong looked behind him. Irvine's wing was almost overlapping as it should be. He tightened his safety belt. "Here goes," he said to himself, pushed over and into the dive, out of the sun and on the down wind some 14,000 feet.

A cool satisfaction possessed Strong. He'd never found himself steadier. As he dove, he studied the planes on the carrier deck and knew they would go up like tinder. He looked at the red circle. "Nice of them to give me a bull's-eye."

Garlow, Strong's radioman and gunner, had his mind on other things. He was riding down backwards, unable to see the carrier. He kept looking for bumps from AA fire. "I thought I was squirrel fodder."

From the gentle rock of the plane Garlow knew that Strong had released the bomb and was pulling steeply out of his dive. In his excitement, Strong had forgotten to open the flaps of the plane. And then, impudence of impudence, Strong swept low and strafed the port side of the giant carrier, pouring his ammunition in her gun positions. Of course that is good tactics—it left less guns to fire at him.

Garlow, looking back on the carrier, got a good view of the destruction their bomb caused and shouted into the microphone: "There's a big black cloud of smoke coming out of her deck, with flames in it. Holy Moses, there goes Irvine's—I mean Mr. Irvine's! He hit her, too, smack near the circle."

Garlow, however, had little time to gloat. The AA tracer fire he expected was now pouring into him. Worse, a dozen Zeros jumped the two planes. Apparently they'd been flying close to the water waiting for a torpedo plane attack. Japs are scared of torpedoes!

The first Zero made a permanent mistake. After a burst, he turned his belly to Garlow. Garlow dropped him in the water, and as he crashed, he burst into flame. Then Irvine's gunner, Eligie Williams, got a Jap, too.

The two pilots, sideslipping, hopping and skimming the whitecaps, weren't making the shooting easy for their gunners.

Now that he had had his revenge, now that he had dumped a bomb smack on a Jap carrier, Strong considered his chances of getting back pretty slim, so he opened up on his radio and sent in: "This is Strong. Strong and Irvine. We got two hits on a Jap carrier of the *Shokaku* class. Her position is zed, her course zed, her speed zed."

He didn't have time to amplify that report. The ten Zeros

were making it too hard for them. At least twenty passes had been made at them, their planes were shot full of holes and still the Japs kept coming. The Japs followed 20, 30, 40, and then 50 miles. Strong opened up his radio again to report two hits on the carrier and its position. He wanted Air Officer Crommelin to know that he had delivered. Then not far ahead of him, he saw a cloud down low. He yelled to Irvine to get into it and the two of them flew for the cloud. It shook off the Japs and the two men for the first time were out of danger.

In the blessed safety of the cloud Irvine said to his gunner, Williams, "I feel like a smoke; what about you?" "You bet," said Williams, and they had one.

Stretching their fuel, the two pilots made the *Enterprise*. Fortunately the *Enterprise* was steaming into the wind and Signal Officer Lindsey brought them in at once. They had less than ten gallons between them.

"Personally, I don't see how in the world you got away with it, Strong," Commander Crommelin said in congratulating the pilots and gunners. "The two of you took on the biggest part of Tojo's carrier fleet." Looking about him he added: "What about your gunners?"

"They got a Jap each out of a dozen that followed us, sir," said Strong. Crommelin shoved his hand through a big hole in Irvine's plane: "What's this doing here?"

Eligie Williams, Irvine's gunner, spoke up: "I'm sorry, sir. I believe that I'll be able to do better next time." Irvine said: "Eligie had missed breakfast and only had an orange before he got into battle."

28. *Then There Was One*

The *Hornet* was hit by two torpedoes about 9:30 on the morning of October 26. The Japs crippled the ship but did not sink her. They continued to attack, even as the wounded and sick were lowered over the ship's side to assisting destroyers. At nearly 3 in the afternoon the ship was taken in tow, but 45 minutes later another wave of attacking planes came in. Finally at 4:11 the Japs scored further torpedo hits and the explosions resulting from these were fatal. The order to abandon ship came at 4:30; there was comparatively little loss of life. That evening as the ship lay dead in the water listing heavily to starboard, the decision to sink her was made. Once more, one of our destroyers had the sad job of sinking an American carrier. At moonrise the *Hornet*, last of the carrier toll suffered by our fleet during the first year of war, settled beneath the Pacific.

Lieutenant Commander William J. Widhelm of the *Hornet* told of the Jap fleet retreat three days later in the wardroom of the Big E. With his rear-seatman, Gus Widhelm had made a forced landing near the Jap carriers and watched the Jap fleet steam by within spitting distance. His face was still an angry red from the two-day exposure.

Gus had led a dive bomber attack from the *Hornet* on the Jap carrier. First they saw a Jap cruiser force about 150 miles out, obviously bait. "Dime a dozen, these cans," he told his section leader, Ben Moore, who was later to return to the *Enterprise* with a mean fragment wound in his neck.

Next they sighted a force of two battleships, a heavy cruiser, one light cruiser, and several destroyers. "Still chicken feed, but getting better," he said.

A dozen Jap Zeros contested their way at this point and Widhelm's fighter protection evaporated. So Widhelm flew on with fifteen Douglas dive bombers. His hunch was right. Forty miles further he found two large Jap carriers with a protective screen of ten cruisers and destroyers. "And with them a whole flock of Zeros," he added.

"Passing through that cloudful of Zeros I collected two," he said. "Then four minutes from my dive approach point a cagey Jap put a shot into my engine, tearing up my oil line." Gus is one of the Navy's best pilots, but he admitted this Jap was his match. "Even though the temperature did go up, I figured I could reach the Japs to deliver my TNT. I knew that I was a dead duck anyway—so what the hell."

As he fully expected, the oil pressure dropped. He crowded the plane but when he could not maintain altitude he reluctantly turned the lead over to his number two man, Ben Moore, thinking that he might glide in following their attack by taking advantage of the ensuing Jap excitement.

"When I saw that I couldn't glide in with my bomb, I went into a vertical dive, making about 300 knots. At 3,000 feet I shucked my bomb and pulled out and then climbed to put the most distance possible between us and the Jap fleet. On the way out I saw a large Jap carrier of the *Shokaku* class smoking through two deck holes and traveling slow, while the other was making frantic maneuvers to avoid Ben's bombers.

"That smoke must have been coming from the bomb holes Strong and Irvine made at least an hour earlier.

"I then saw eleven of my boys pour six 1,000-pound bombs into the carrier of the *Zuikaku* class with one near miss which can often be better than a hit. The Jap AA barrage isn't a patch on what our ships throw up," Gus added contemptuously.

"The big 1,000-pounders peeled the deck back like skinning a banana, and the ship burst into flames.

"My radioman, George Stokely, said: 'This is better than sitting up in heaven.'"

When about 200 feet off the water and about 15 miles from the carriers, the two men lost sight of the burning Jap carriers although they could still see smoke. When the plane hit the water the two men leaped out of their cockpits with parachutes, rubber boats, and chart board which included maps, and prepared to make the best of a tough situation.

They were getting squared away in their tiny quarters when two Jap battleships approached about 4 miles distant. They also saw several carrier Zeros crash into the water near the Jap destroyers which were convoying the battleships.

"Those chicks just naturally didn't have a brood hen to go to," he said. "Their carriers were too badly hit."

Widhelm and Stokely stayed in the water for about an hour trying to swim and tow the rubber boat. "It was bad trying to make ourselves look small," said Widhelm, who is a husky six-footer with shoulders about as wide as he is long.

When the Jap ships went hull down over the curving horizon, the men got back into the boat, but not for long. About thirty minutes later a Jap destroyer appeared followed by a cruiser, and Gus and Stokely slipped into the water again.

The destroyer saw them and changed course. As they approached, groups of "toothy, grinning Japs stood alongside the rail and laughed at our plight," Gus said and added: "A Jap seaman got a line to throw over to us but an officer approached him and he went away." Widhelm added: "It's just as well that the seaman didn't throw the line because Stokely and I had agreed not to take it."

Next came a cruiser. It had been hit aft and its guns were blown clear. The plane and catapult were fused into one mess that looked like a Dali creation.

The two men were getting used to Jap ships now. The next two steamed within hailing distance and saw them, but made no effort to shoot the Americans, leaving them instead to the ravages of sun, hunger, and thirst.

That was the last the two men saw of the Jap fleet with the exception of one Jap Zero float plane which flew toward them about 3 miles and turned and headed away looking for Jap pilot survivors.

Widhelm and Stokely settled down to spend a long time on their South Sea cruise. They rationed their food for thirty days with a thimbleful of water an hour after sundown to hold in their mouths to create saliva.

Three days later when Widhelm came aboard the *Enterprise* he said: "There we were sitting on the broad Pacific, and Stokely had rigged a mast and we'd made a sail of our parachute—and we were off to find the bare-breasted maidens of the Stewart Islands, when a damn PBY had to find us."

While "Sea Bees" were repairing the *Enterprise* wounds from the Santa Cruz battle, the Japs moved down to take Guadalcanal. Admiral Halsey, newly appointed commander in chief of the South Pacific, gave orders to proceed to Guadalcanal. The Sea Bees did not have time to vacate the ship.

The Big E maneuvered south of Guadalcanal, holding her air force in readiness. She was the only carrier left in the South Pacific.

6

NOVEMBER 13, 1942–JUNE, 1943

29. *Turning the Tide*

Knowing that we had but one carrier, and that badly damaged, the Japs quickly reorganized a surface striking force to move into the Solomons. For the Japs it was an ABC maneuver. Battleships, cruisers, and destroyers would lay out 250 miles beyond reach of our small Guadalcanal airforce. Then late in the afternoon, they would steam in at high speed for a devastating night shelling with which they intended to destroy the airfield and decimate our Marines. The bombardment was to be followed with troop landings.

On the afternoon of November 12, twenty-five Jap torpedo planes (almost certainly from a Jap carrier) and eight fighters were searching for the *Enterprise* south of Guadalcanal. They did not find us.

Instead, they located an American cruiser screening force and some American transports off Guadalcanal. Only three Zeros, reportedly, flew away from that attack. One of the thirty shot down crash-dived the cruiser *San Francisco*.

That same night the Japs sent in a mighty armada. The hopelessly outmatched American force, however, gave battle. Three destroyers led the attack. Typical was the work of the already damaged *San Francisco*. While helping blow up a Jap cruiser, she engaged a destroyer and sank it. Then with

149

the other vessels she closed in on a Jap battleship and hit it eighteen times at 2,000 yards. The other American destroyers and cruisers making the same run were not hit by Jap shell fire.

Aboard the *Enterprise* next morning, Friday, November 13, two hours before daybreak Lieutenant (j.g.) Robert D. Gibson was wakened.

Gibson was a tall, soft-spoken, blue-eyed flier from Unionville, Missouri. He had had an excellent musical training and could play anything from a French horn to a piccolo. His flying and fighting, like his ability to play the piano, were first rate.

Bob took off at daybreak with Clifford E. Schindele, his rear-seatman.

Maybe Bob was thinking of other crucial hops he had taken, all on beautiful clear days like this. He had been on the *Yorktown* in the Midway battle. In the August 24 and October 26 battles, he had flown off on the *Enterprise*. Or he may have been thinking of his father, a monument dealer, from whom he learned the trade.

At any rate, he flew to the end of his search sector. He was not satisfied with that and radioed his wingman, Ensign Buchanan. "I know damn well that there are Japs around here. I can smell them. Let's stretch her some more," he said.

"Roger," said Buchanan, accepting.

Gibson and Buchanan were rewarded. The two pilots looked to the south of the New Georgia island group and there, 150 miles west of Guadalcanal, big as life, was a cruiser force of eleven ships—three light cruisers, three heavy cruisers and five destroyers.

Gibson flew on and verified the contact. As the *Enterprise* was maintaining radio silence and could not answer him, Bob remained over the large Jap force for an hour and a half, amplifying his report, giving speed, course, and direction.

Shortly thereafter, Pilots Martin D. Carmody and his wingman Halloran located a transport group to the north of the island in the strait between New Georgia and Santa Isabel. They too stretched their search.

While flying over the Japs, Gibson made eight separate reports on the disposition and composition of the Jap force while the Japs in turn threw up everything they had to drive him away.

Finally, with their gas supply running low, Gibson and Buchanan climbed to 17,000 feet. They had plenty of time to weigh the consequences. Carefully they selected their targets, a heavy cruiser of the *Nachi* class.

"Here goes," Gibson called to Buchanan. He put his plane into a steep dive, with Buchanan following by seconds.

"The explosion," according to rear-seatman Schindele, "picked up the whole ship and set it over about six feet." Then as Gibson pulled out, Schindele strafed until they got out of range. After that he turned his camera on the burning ship.

Meanwhile, Buchanan got a direct hit too and between them they left the heavy cruiser burning fiercely and dead in the water.

Gibson then radioed the Big E—the first attack word received of the day's successful action. When it was relayed over the loudspeaker system, *Enterprise* men cheered.

By now the two pilots were almost out of gas. Making a quick calculation, Gibson called Guadalcanal and said that he would try to land there but added that the two planes would probably land in the water.

The two men flew on with reduced throttle, nursing the little gas that remained. When the field finally came into view, they saw that a Jap raid was under way. Despite this, marines opened the field and the two men came in for a landing, without circling. Now for the first time, Gibson learned that Buchanan's plane had been badly hit and that the plane had no rudder control. As Buchanan landed, the plane ran off the runway, jumped two ditches, and swerved past a crumpled Jap plane, but he kept the plane upright.

As soon as the Jap planes departed from their raid on Guadalcanal, Gibson asked that his plane be refueled and armed. He and Schindele took off from Henderson Field within twenty-five minutes with a squadron of Marine pilots to attack the transport group again which had been reported by Lieutenant Carmody of the *Enterprise*.

Zeros notwithstanding, Gibson got a hit on a medium-sized transport of about 8,000 tons. "I did not notice the troops on it," he said, "until we got in close because the ship's color and their clothes blended. They were close packed."

During their departure Schindele shot down a Zero and then once again took pictures which showed the transport burning fiercely.

Not satisfied with that, Gibson and Schindele returned to Guadalcanal, armed, gassed, and returned to complete the destruction. This time he flew with seven other *Enterprise* pilots. As they got to the Jap transport force there were but six ships left and two of them were dead in the water. Others farther up the channel were burning.

As they prepared for the attack, a large force of Jap Zeros intercepted them.

Gibson's airplane was badly damaged and it went out of control temporarily, the plane falling like a dead duck.

"I was hit and had to fall out," said Gibson. "As I was falling I managed to release my bomb. Then I got my controls back. But just as I pulled out, a Zero got on my wing. He rode on it for ten miles, giving me bursts. My rear guns were jammed so the Zero didn't have any opposition. As a matter of fact, he was flying in formation on me, perhaps 100 feet off. Finally he either ran out of ammunition or got disgusted and headed for home. Anyway, he didn't do much damage. He only knocked out my control cable and put a few holes in my plane."

Gibson's squadron commander, Lieutenant Commander John A. Thomas, corrected that one. "A few holes! God Almighty! Every one of your tanks was punctured and the sides of your fuselage were riddled!"

Meanwhile, two long overdue fighter pilots were trying to return to the *Enterprise*. While escorting five bombers the pair had chased off two Zeros and in the dogfight lost their bearing. They were hopelessly lost in the vast Pacific, an hour's gas remained and darkness was rushing in.

Chip Reding called the other pilot, Hank Leder: "Looks like the duty yeoman won't have to rout us out tomorrow morning, two hours before sunrise."

"I'd rather he would," said Leder.

Then, suddenly, Reding asked: "Hey, aren't those wakes down there off to our starboard?"

They looked. "Suppose they are Japs?"

Gas-stingy, the men circled slowly, hating to give altitude. But sure enough, those wakes were all attached to warships and those warships upon closer inspection were friendly. There was no carrier, but one of them was the *South Dakota*, which had been detached from the *Enterprise* screen the night before.

Crash-landing in the water to be picked up by a destroyer was out of the question: fighter planes were mighty scarce out on our front at this time and these two must be saved at all costs.

Leder did the bright thing. "Please point your ships," he wrote in a message drop, "in the direction of our carrier."

Soon the huge ships and their escort, a-flutter with signal

pennants, changed course and Leder and Reding took their bearings, wagged their wings for a "thanks" and were slicing the breeze for home.

Signal Officer Daniels gave them a cut on the first approach just before dark. They landed with about a helmet full of gas between them and two grinning faces.

30. 50,000 *Tons*

In the afternoon of November 13, it was learned that a Japanese battleship force was on its way to bombard Guadalcanal. They came within 10 miles of Savo Island and within twenty minutes would have been in shelling distance of Henderson Field.

Lieutenant Albert P. Coffin, taking off from the Big E with his nine torpedo pilots, was told to proceed 300 miles north and attack any suitable targets with his torpedoes. But Coffin decided to stretch the route by way of Savo Island and 10 miles north of the island sighted the Jap battleship force. He didn't hesitate about his decision. He did not ask for fighter protection.

Taking advantage of cloud cover, Coffin and eight of his nine pilots climbed for position, divided and then swooped down from opposite sides for the kill. But before they came in, the ninth pilot, Lieutenant Boudreaux flew in singly to divert AA fire from the slow torpedo planes. While the Japs were firing at Boudreaux, the split torpedo squadron hit simultaneously from both sides. That attack was the most successful in U. S. torpedo attack history. Three columns of water funneled into the air as torpedoes sank into the ship's vitals. There was explosion after explosion and the giant *Kongo* class battleship stopped dead in the water.

Each of the nine planes received at least one AA hit but not one man was injured and not one plane was lost.

In subsequent attacks from Guadalcanal, eight torpedo hits were made on the battleship by these same pilots and when last seen in the evening there was a fire in her stern, men were abandoning the ship, and next morning an oil slick two miles in diameter was all that remained.

The Japs later confirmed the sinking of the battleship on Radio Tokyo. This is the first Jap battleship, so far as is known, that was sunk by carrier-borne planes.

In addition to the battleship, the nine pilots made three torpedo hits on a cruiser of the *Mogami* class and four on Japanese transports loaded with perhaps a division (15,000 men) of amphibious troops.

Then, two days later, Lieutenant Coffin and his lads dropped bombs and Molotov breadbaskets on beached Jap transports and Jap ground positions.

Four of the torpedo pilots were former students of Lieutenant Coffin's, who taught at the Navy's Corpus Christi Training Center. Lieutenant Boudreaux said of his teacher: "He did right well for himself."

Boudreaux was right. In three days Skipper Coffin took part in six destructive missions made by Big E planes operating from now "secure" Henderson Field. However, Coffin disclaims all praise and gives the credit for the three-day destruction of more than 50,000 tons of Jap tonnage to the skill of the nine fliers and to the Marine fighter pilots who gave them protection.

Lieutenant Bobby Edwards (Thomas E. Edwards, Jr., of Wichita Falls, Texas) was in a New Caledonia hospital more than 800 miles away when his *Enterprise* shipmates started pounding the Japs off Guadalcanal. His knee was badly swollen, almost three times its natural size.

A Marine sergeant kept him posted and when he told Edwards of the big battle shaping and how the Japs were moving down, Bobby bribed the sergeant to slip him some clothes and he thumbed a ride to the airfield. There he found a cargo plane just taking off. He stopped it, saying he was a fighter pilot off the *Enterprise*, needed at Guadalcanal. The transport pilot agreed: "Anyone who can fly a plane is needed there, brother. You're good for a triple A priority as far as I'm concerned."

Once at Henderson Field, Bobby swiped a jeep and drove it to a gassed and armed fighter plane which belonged to a Marine major. Bobby climbed in and took off.

On the way out, Bobby saw a Zero and shot him down. Then he was jumped by seven Zeros with all of them making separate runs on him. When he managed to get one of them smoking, they all ducked—perhaps out of ammunition. One, however, turned back and that was bad because Bobby was now out of ammunition.

Just as in the movies, another Big E fighter showed up and Bobby radioed him: "Hey, take this lug off my neck. I'm out of ammunition."

"Wilco," said the pilot and took care of the Jap.

Waiting for Edwards when he came down were Fighter Skipper Flatley and the major whose plane had been taken.

The major talked first. "We appreciate your aggressiveness, young man, but I needed that plane for my next flight."

Edwards looked like the little boy caught with jam on his hands. He said nothing.

Later, the major told Flatley: "We need more like him in the air."

Three days later, Bobby was evacuated to a hospital on another island. But, with a Jap scalp under his belt, "it was easier to take," he said.

✦

Lieutenant Goddard's peacetime forest ranger training out of Bemidji, Minnesota, stood him in good stead at Guadalcanal.

On November 15, after three Jap ships had been run aground so that their supplies might be salvaged and men landed, three Big E pilots went out to smack them some more.

Gibson and Stevens led the attack and after they got three good explosions which started large fires, Goddard decided to find himself a new target.

He cruised over the Jap positions carefully. He studied the lay of the land and circled and strafed a position that looked like a machine-gun nest but he held on to his bomb. Then he saw a place which looked just right. No Japs were in sight but he thought he saw faint paths leading to the beached ships and one little path leading back to some large trees. He decided it was a dumping ground and dropped his bomb.

He hit the jackpot. The bomb exploded and in turn there was explosion after explosion along a quarter-mile chain. Apparently a fuel or ammunition dump had been hit.

Fires, hundreds of feet high, kept burning all day and that night. Next morning a huge column of black smoke was still pouring up from about a half-mile long stretch.

31. A Seventy-three Hour Swim

Ensign Jefferson "Tiny" Carroum of Smackover, Arkansas, put up a magnificent fight for his life after the November battle of Guadalcanal. He's perhaps the smallest pilot in the Navy. He stretched to make the required five feet four, and he weighed about 120 pounds before his ordeal.

Tiny took off from the Big E with a 1,000-pound bomb to hit the cruisers Gibson and Buchanan had reported. Tiny found them, got a near miss—about 20 feet—and then hustled back to Guadalcanal to reload.

Loaded, he went back to have a try at the transports. At 9,000 feet within 5 miles of the Jap ships a flock of Zeros hit him. He managed to squeeze through and by this time was in diving position.

"I peeled off, going down real steep, with a Jap sitting on my tail," he said. "On my way down I turned over on my back to avoid him, and with corkscrewing managed to get on the biggest transport in the middle of a convoy of eight ships—about 12,000 tons and loaded with troops. I released at 1,500, getting a hit amidship.

"On the pullout I caught AA from a cruiser and two destroyers; AA hit my engine. It started smoking a little and then a Zero was right on, making runs on me.

"As I pulled up to fire at the Zero, smoke and oil were coming out of my engine so bad that I couldn't see him very well, so I stuck my head out of the cockpit and fired from that position until my engine quit cold. I nosed over and saw that I was only 100 feet from the water. I didn't have time to get my landing flaps down and I saw I was cross-wind which was not so good. I hit hard, but I think I got the Zero.

"When I hit I was knocked out. The next thing I remember the water was coming up around my knees. I unstrapped my safety belt and then crawled out on the wing. My radio-man already had the life raft out and was about to inflate it, I saw; so I yelled: 'Hynson, don't inflate it. The Zeros will strafe us.' Then I passed out again. As I came to, the nose of the plane was starting down. As the tail went down it caught the life raft with it and something on the life raft caught my gunbelt and pulled me under the water. I managed to unbuckle the belt and then pulled the zipper of my life jacket. It inflated and jerked me up to the air.

"I don't remember anything for about fifteen minutes after. You see, I got a wallop.

"As we were coasting along in our life jackets, hoping to get picked up, I asked my radioman how many men he supposed we had killed, because the only satisfaction within sight was the flames from the burning transport we hit and the glowing spots on the horizon where five other Jap coffins were burning. Hynson's mind, though, was on the sharks which had already tasted human meat in those waters. It wasn't much good trying to keep his mind off them.

"Then I said: 'Come on; let's start swimming. I saw an island when we went down.'

"I got him to take his shoes off and then he pulled his pants and underwear off too. Then we began swimming to those islands some 25 miles off.

"We swam about four hours. Then a Jap destroyer came by. He was going toward Guadalcanal and missed us about 50 yards, but it was already dark by then.

"My radioman wasn't a good swimmer. He wanted to stop and rest and take it easy. I'd swim ahead and make him catch me. Then I'd leave him again.

"We swam until 1 A.M. Then a rain squall came up and the stars were covered. That was bad because the stars I had lined up were blanked out. So, we had to swim by the wind. It was from the east and we were going south. My radioman wanted to go downwind, but I called him back.

"By five o'clock in the morning the next day we could barely see the islands as the long slow swells lifted us. We hadn't made much progress.

"When daylight came on, we could see real good and that got us to swimming a little better. About 10 A.M. a good swell lifted me where I could see and I thought I saw a reef. So I yelled back to Hynson: 'There's a reef about 200 yards ahead.'

" 'Go ahead and get it,' he said, 'and bring help. I'm too tired to make it.'

"But we swam on a couple of more hours and it didn't get any closer. I realized then that my reef was an island, and about ten miles away.

"I turned around to my radioman and called him but he was too weak to answer. Then I decided that to save us I would have to swim off and try to make it to shore and bring back help.

"I planned to make the island by 4 that afternoon. As the swells lifted me I could even see what looked like native huts.

"But I swam and swam until it was almost dark but I got hardly any closer because the current was strong. I drifted some and tried to swim a little crossways and drift and so perhaps hit another island.

"The current seemed to quit for a time so I struck out strong again. I swam until about 1 o'clock that night. Then I bumped into a coconut. I thought how good it would be to eat. I was hungry and thirsty, being thirty hours out. I would have given anything to have had it to drink. I grabbed hold of it and pushed it in front of me as I swam, thinking that maybe the island I would reach might not have any food. And I thought, too, it might give me buoyancy.

"And after thinking about drinking the milk, I wished I could sleep. Then the current started again so I had to turn loose of the coconut and swim right out strong.

"Then I lit out with a resolve that I would make the island and I gave it as much strength as I had. But I saw I was making little headway.

"I got so exhausted that I could only stay awake by ducking my head under the water, and then the water would get in my nose and throat and ears and I was just too damn dry and thirsty to spit it out.

"I felt that if I couldn't make it to the island by the second morning I never would make it during the day with the hot sun out. That made me panicky and gave me strength to swim a little harder.

"I passed out two or three times from exhaustion. When I'd come around I'd talk out loud and tell myself that that island was life or death and I had to make it. I told myself I was a cheap specimen if I could come so close to land and couldn't get closer.

"After a while even that argument left me and I slipped off to sleep. Along about 4 in the morning, I passed out completely. I had a nightmare and woke up yelling for one of my flying mates—'Hoogerwoof, get me out of here. Hooger, get me out of this glass swimming cage; I'm freezing to death.'

"My teeth were chattering up and down. I was awake for about fifteen minutes before I realized that I was in the ocean. Finally, I realized where I was and could see the island. I started swimming again.

"But I was just too weak to swim against the current. I made up my mind to change islands and drifted along with the current. As I swam small fish came all around me. One got under my life jacket and it scared me because I thought it was a shark, and I swam harder.

"Finally I swam down current and it took me to the middle of a lagoon. I could see some smoke and native huts. I couldn't see any villages on any other small islands. I had heard that there were Japs around. I didn't want to end the second day (after forty-eight hours) with a Jap waiting for me to crawl up to him.

"My face swelled so that my eyes were almost closed. I tried to use one at a time to see where I was heading. Then when I closed one eye too long, I couldn't get it open again. The sun had just burned it shut. So I used the one eye to swim with.

"I swam continuously then until about 7 P.M., when it was getting dark. It was raining and that felt pretty good, but the wind went against me, and by 10 o'clock that night I passed out again and was carried out of the bay.

"I woke next morning about 10 o'clock. At first I couldn't get my second eye open. I was having nightmares again and after one dream about fresh water I drank three swallows. I realized then I was drinking salt water which woke me up quick. I ducked my head under the water to wash my eyes and get them open and finally got one a little open so I had a slit to look out of. I saw that the wind was now taking me right again, so I swam downwind, hoping that I could make land by 7 that night, my third.

"Looking through the slit I had for an eye showed me that I was getting closer so I worked hard. Being the third day in the water without water or food I knew that if I wouldn't make it, I was lost.

"And then, at about 7 P.M., I got to the last 200 yards. I dropped my legs and saw that the water was only waist deep but had a sharp coral bottom. I cut my feet kicking against the coral and I tried to walk but every time I raised my shoulders they were too heavy. I just couldn't hold them up. So I half swam, half walked, cutting my hands and feet some more but I knew that I was making it and was safe.

"About 50 yards from shore the water was only a foot deep. There I had to walk. I tried to but fell and I had to go on my hands and knees. I got up on land finally, and could only crawl about 10 feet from the water." This was seventy-three hours after he was shot down.

"I lay there and rolled over on my back. As I rolled over I managed to get away from the beach where I found a mud-hole. It must have been from the rain that afternoon. I drank all I wanted and then it rained most of the night, but it didn't bother me. I woke up near daylight shivering and my teeth clattering. But I didn't worry then. I knew it would soon be clear and warm and daylight. Best of all I wouldn't have to swim."

Next morning Tiny was waked by natives shouting. He could not get his eyes open to see them but he felt for his pilot's license and showed that to them. They carried him into a canoe and took him to a village eight miles away where they bathed him and dressed his wounds and fed him rice and hot tea.

To be taken from the middle of the war to a quiet native village such as this one was heaven. Tiny spent much of his time in a Church of England chapel where the natives took him each day at sunup and sundown. Sunday was given wholly over to meditation and chewing of sugar cane.

Before the PBY picked Tiny up in ten days, they gave him a party. An old horn-type Victrola played over and over their one record, *How-Do-You-Do, Everybody, How-Do-You-Do*, the girls danced, and the evening was given over to the chief who quizzed Tiny about tanks and submarines.

32. *Salute to Rear-seatmen*

Dark, thin-faced Earl Gallagher was an aviation radioman third class. He and his pilot, Ensign Paul M. Halloran, did not come back from the November 14 battle. They had been assigned a search sector off Guadalcanal. They received a contact report of an enemy cruiser and destroyer force coming "down the slot" and went far beyond the return limits of their gasoline. They found the enemy, fought off a swarm of attacking Zeros, scored a bomb hit on a cruiser and set it on fire. Then they tried to reach home base, but their fuel did not hold out. Their normal call of duty required them to complete their search and return to the carrier. The last

word heard from the two men was the pilot calling an un-
seen wingman: "Where in hell are you?"

Because one does not hear much about rear-seatmen, I had
planned to write a story about Earl before he was lost. For
the most part one reads only about the pilots and not about
the men who ride with them. Unfortunately, these unsung
heroes are seldom decorated.

In general, rear-seatmen are a drab-looking lot. They are
usually seen in dungarees or coveralls, generally have grease
under their fingernails and when gathered in the ready room
often look like a huddled group of miners getting ready to
go into the hole.

Earl was different, mostly due to his driving ambition to
be a pilot. He had been in the Navy eighteen months and
spent his spare time on the hangar deck learning about engines; in the aviation ordnance room learning about guns; in
radio repair learning about radios. Combined with his ambition, the lad had the knack of looking on the bright side. The
closer the *Enterprise* approached action, the more ready his
humor. He was good medicine.

When Earl came up for his physical, he learned that he
had a hernia and could never be a dive bomber pilot. Without hesitation, he went to the doctor and arranged for an
operation. That was unsuccessful—he still could not pass.
Undeterred, he underwent another and this time the muscles
healed, and he passed. He would never let on that it hurt him.

Within a short time, Earl excelled in his many duties. When
I asked Air Group Commander Dick Gaines for an outstanding rear-seatman, he said: "See Earl Gallagher. He's good."

Before I had time to finish my notes for the story, we were
in the second battle of Guadalcanal and Earl did not come
back. Hence, I went to one of his many friends—Ferdinand
John Sugar of Webster, Massachusetts—and asked him the
questions I had prepared for Earl.

"Well, we gunners are as responsible as our pilots in seeing that our plane delivers its bombload and returns from whatever mission may be assigned," said Sugar.

"We've got to check up on last-minute changes of rendezvous orders. The drift of the plane. Keep our radios functioning. See that there is nothing loose in the plane for the dive. Exchange proper recognition signals. This and a thousand other things.

"For personal qualities, the rear-seatman must have guts—like Earl. That fellow was scared of absolutely nothing. Sitting backwards from the direction of flight is not easy. You sit there and wait for it. Your life is in your pilot's hands and you have to trust him. You cannot see your danger and plan to cope with it. You have nothing to do, essentially, about saving your neck. You see the red streaks of tracers squirting past and you sit tight and hope that none of the AA bursts are going to hit you. As the plane builds up speed, you hope the pilot will release the bomb properly and pull out of his dive. All the while you keep your eyes peeled for Zeros and, when they come, you have to throw bursts at them while your pilot is pitching the plane around taking evasive action.

"But there is yet a bigger problem which is harder to describe. You must fit yourself to the pilot. You have no choice. And sometimes, you get a bad draw—not all pilots are equally good. But regardless you clear your mind of all doubts about his flying ability during landing and take-offs, dog fights while on combat patrol, or diving on enemy ships.

"To achieve this confidence, a very close relationship—a oneness—must grow between you and your pilot. What rough spots come up, you iron out after each flight. This should never be discussed with others.

"Then you must be good with a gun. Earl was good. During his last attack, he held off seven Zeros and his pilot was able to smack the bomb home into that Jap cruiser—and their life work was done.

"To be a good gunner requires cool nerve and hard-gripping hands. Nerve for sitting up there waiting for the Japs to get into range even though their guns are firing at you and you haven't the armor protection the pilot has. And hard-gripping hands because you cannot let the gun grips get out of your hands, even though your plane is bucking and the hood is open and the slipstream is strong and there is danger of falling out."

He kept coming back to Earl, his friend whom he had lost the week before. "Gallagher had all these qualities. And remember how nicely bronzed his face was? Keeping fit was part of his flying."

I asked: "How did you feel, Sugar, on your last attack?"

He laughed. "You mean do I get scared? Well, there isn't much fear once you leave your ship and it fades out of sight. When it melts into the horizon you know that you are on your own and something new in life is about to happen.

"When you get the radio contact report of the enemy's position, you're set. You've been waiting for this. But gradually, in spite of yourself, you tense up. It usually gets cold when you climb for your dive and you aren't sure whether it is the cold in the air that is making the goose pimples or your fear. Then you wonder what makes you shake clear inside.

"Then you push over and ride down backwards looking up into the sky for Zeros to pounce down on you.

"When the AA comes whizzing past it doesn't bother you much because you're traveling too fast and you've got your gun and you're hanging on to it with might and main.

"After that the bomb is dropped and you make a hit—and you know your pilot is just as good as you knew he was. You have a feeling that your life work is completed.

"You rock with the AA and streak over the water and suddenly it comes to you that you're safe—you've got a chance to get out.

"Then, once you spot your carrier and see it's still up, everything comes normal. But to get that down deep, ever-lasting feeling in your heart, you've got to experience it yourself."

Most pilots give plenty of credit to their rear-seatmen. When Lieutenant Carmody of San Jose, California, came aboard the carrier after the November 13-16 fight, for example, he told me: "Don't give me the credit. I'm here today because my rear-seatman John Liska (of Van Nuys, California) brought me back. Six Zeros attacked us and he held them off. Would you believe it?" he added, "when the first Zero came in, Liska, polite as always, says: 'Mr. Carmody, there is a Zero coming in on our tail.'

"Then the next day when our plane went down, it was Liska who fixed our radio in the dark and sent in our position, and saved our necks. If decorations are handed out, Liska ought to come first."

Remembering that remark, I asked a rear-seat gunner, two weeks after the battle, what he thought when decorations were being given to pilots.

"It's like this with us enlisted gunners," he said. "We assemble on the flight deck which is still scarred up from accidents some of us had with our pilots. We stand proudly, knowing that we fought a good fight and that some will be recognized for what they did, and hoping, of course, that we have not been forgotten.

"We see our pilots step forward, salute, and get their awards pinned on by the admiral. We are just as glad as the next man to see our pilots decorated. We know how much guts their job takes.

"We think: 'There are still four more pilots. After the offi-cers get their decorations, we'll be next.'

"Our minds, naturally enough, go over the battle and we think of the action in which we fought side by side with these pilots. We think of our fellow radiomen—some who did not come back—and wish they had.

"Like Edwards (of Bristol, Vermont) who shot down two Zeros while wounded and died before his plane landed. And Teyshack (of Streator, Illinois) who was wounded in the Solomons battle when a Jap shell exploded in his cockpit and his guns jammed but yet who freed those guns while under the fire of Jap Zeros and drove them off.

"And Sugar, who has flown for more than 2,300 hours in dive bombers and helped Bob Dixon make that famous phrase live, 'Scratch one flattop,' because he was Dixon's rear-seat gunner and shot down attacking Zeros.

"And Ralph Gowling (of Los Angeles) who risked his life to lug his wounded pilot out of their rapidly sinking plane and got him into a life raft, and took care of him, and after two days paddling without letup, brought him safely to a tiny island where they were picked up by patrol craft.

"And then, as you think of these things, the last pilot has saluted and received his decoration and you get tense and your breath comes hard and you are hoping to the last second that you'll be surprised and called up because you feel that you deserve a decoration.

"But then we are dismissed and fall out. And for a second some rather wild thoughts keep pounding inside. 'I flew with him. I was in that attack. I helped bring him back. Didn't I take all that he did?'

"But after a while, that is forgotten. You remember that the pilot is the captain of the ship and there remains the hope: 'I'm lucky. I've got a good pilot. We're flying again. Maybe the next time, I'll get a decoration too.'"

For more than one-and-a-half years of war, Navy rear-seatmen were not even given aviation wings to wear. Finally, in the summer of 1943, the combat crew insignia was issued—silver wings with settings for combat action stars up to a maximum of three.

Esprit de corps is much more than a matter of wings, but such things certainly help. Naval aviation combat crews have all the spirit as individuals that is needed: a finer lot of men does not exist in any of the armed services. They are gradually getting the recognition they deserve, including an increase in decorations. They deserve every one they get.

33. *Praying Helps*

When I think of the *Enterprise*, I think of men. There's Lieutenant Commander James Henry Flatley, for example, fighting squadron commander. Jimmy is one of the Navy's best fliers. In some 4,000 hours he has yet to put a scratch on a plane. Men like to fly for him. With Lieutenant Commander John Smith Thach of *Yorktown* fame, Flatley devised new tactical methods of shooting down the Zero.

At the outset of the war, Jimmy knew that there were speedier and more maneuverable fighters than our carrier-based Grummans. However, after Midway he was the first person to say that the Grumman could out-fight the Zero if it were properly flown and fought.

"Our pre-war tactics were wrong. We concentrated too much on individual training and dive bombing. We failed to conceive of a combat team. Hence, when *Enterprise* planes met the Japs over Pearl Harbor our fighter squadrons were almost totally unprepared for combat with the Jap planes."

After the Midway battle, the morale of the Navy fighter pilots was extremely low. Pilots did not have confidence in their planes. The Zero flew circles around them. This dejection was not helped by the return of only four Marine fliers out of a group of twenty-four who met the Zero.

To help correct this discouraging condition, Flatley addressed a letter to all fighter squadrons pointing out the fallacy of their reasoning and suggesting tactics on which to base future operations.

We must have confidence in our Grumman fighter planes because we have to fight them or we are licked. The advantages of our fire power and armor if properly employed will more than overcome the advantages the Japs enjoy in maneuverability and climb.

After the Coral Sea battle, I asked each pilot if he would trade his Wildcat for a Zero. The answer was: "Well, no. But we have to get more maneuverability and climb to our planes."

That was because they could not overcome the feeling of inferiority because as individuals, operating singly, they could not climb and turn with the Zero.

In order to establish a system of maneuvering that would overcome in part the advantages of maneuverability and climbing, Thach worked out what is now called the Thach Weave, a secret maneuver which prevents the enemy from getting satisfactory aim even though he enjoys all the advantages of initial position. And if the Jap fighter persists, he will be shot down.

Sending out one man, however, to lick a Zero gives him chances of about ten to one against him.

Stay together for mutual protection. The stray plane is a lost plane. The old dogfight of chasing tails must not be employed when opposing a Jap fighter.

The most effective attack against a more maneuverable fighter is to obtain altitude advantage, dive in, attack, and pull up, using speed gained in the dive to maintain altitude advantage. Gain plenty of altitude before contact with the enemy fighters. You can lose altitude fast but you can't gain it fast enough when up against the Zero.

You have a better plane if you handle it properly and in spite of the Zero advantage of maneuverability you can and should shoot them down. The reason for this is your greater fire power and more skillful gunnery.

Don't get excited and rush in. Take your time and make the first attack effective.

Find a cloud if you get in a tough spot.

Any Navy fighter pilot who is willing to give up the armor, the protected fuel tanks or the strength of the Grumman Wildcat for the Zero's greater climb and maneuverability ought to have his head examined.

When Secretary of the Navy Frank Knox read this open letter to fighter pilots, he wrote to Jimmy Flatley:

My dear Commander:

I cannot refrain from expressing my very great admiration for this entire communication and the spirit in which it is written. . . . That is the kind of spirit that wins wars. What we must do in this war, if we are going to win, is not to wait until we have everything exactly as we want it, but rather to do the best with what we have and rely upon those at home to get better equipment to our fighting squadrons just as fast as it is humanly possible to do so.

My warm congratulations and felicitations!

Sincerely yours,

FRANK KNOX

Besides being a brave flier, a good tactician, and an able leader, Jimmy is religious. Saturday night he may be having a game of poker with the boys and drinking Bourbon, but Sunday morning he is in chapel. He believes that a good Christian has more fighting spirit—he's got more to fight for.

We are not a war-like people. We love peace and the fruits of peace. We are fighting heathen enemies who not only seek economic gain, but who would also stamp out Christianity if they are victorious. . . .

Why are we being subjected to this world-wide conflict? The only logical answer is that as Christians we have failed. We have allowed ourselves to become soft. We have disregarded God and

His commandments. Our wills have become weak. Our consciences hardened. We have offended God and as Christian nations are little better than the heathens. We have become hypocrites, professing one thing outwardly and practicing another. . . .

In all of us is the desire to live. It surmounts every other desire. However, we all must die sooner or later. We are fighting now, not so much for our own lives but for the life of our entire nation, for our fathers and mothers, sisters and brothers, our children, for all the millions of Americans who did not ask for this war; who are depending on us; who are daily making sacrifices; who are doing their part to help; who are fighting in all parts of the world for the same thing we are fighting for. As Christians, we should believe that a return to God, through the medium of a few simple prayers, sincerely and humbly said, with a belief in their efficacy, will aid us not only to attain heaven, but will also strengthen us to meet and destroy our enemies fearlessly. . . .

These were the prayers: "Dear God, in your Divine Wisdom, aid and guide the political and military leaders of the United Nations in order that victory may be attained in the shortest possible time." And: "God have mercy on our fighting men wherever they may be. Strengthen them to face death unflinchingly."

To these prayers, Jimmy added:

These prayers are common to all religions. Don't be afraid to say them. Write home and tell your mothers that we're saying them. She taught them to us when we were knee high. She's praying to the same God for our safety right this minute. If we don't like these, say those we know and do like; but pray for strength to do our duty as fighting men, for victory, for forgiveness.

This is not a game. It is the most serious business of our lives. Appealing to God will strengthen us. May God bless us all and hasten our Victory.

34. *Honors*

For the first time in my three continuous months on the Big E, men were in their stiff, uncomfortable Sunday best, dress whites, to receive awards and citations from their skipper, Captain O. B. Hardison, a tall white-haired North Carolinian. Many of their clothes were borrowed because they had lost their gear during the years' bombings.

We were in Noumea harbor. It was a bright day without a cloud in the hot sky. Our ship was swinging easily on the hook responsive to the slight morning breeze blowing off the brown New Caledonia mountains and riffling the harbor water gently. Around us were tankers, crowded transports waiting to go to Guadalcanal, and warships, many with torn eight-inch holes from recent night action in the "Slot" off Guadalcanal. Slowly past us a cargo ship was towed with a ten-foot torpedo hole clear through her middle.

As the men lined up, waiting for Captain Hardison, I overheard a lieutenant mutter: "God damn it, this uniform is choking the living hell out of me. What the devil are we collecting glory for? Our dead shipmates are the heroes."

Captain Hardison stood behind his rostrum. He waited until the noise of four motor torpedo boats blended with the far-away drone of patrol planes. What he said made the men forget about the hole in the ship's side; the tent city in officers' country where rooms had been blown away. Any fear of being a hunted warship was changed to pride in being the lone carrier in the South Pacific.

"Men of the *Enterprise*," said Captain Hardison, "I have called you together to present awards and citations. You have made the *Enterprise* what it is today—the Navy's top fighting ship, a veteran of every carrier action of the war save one,

from the Marshall Islands to the Second Battle of Guadalcanal—two weeks ago."

He looked at the pilots from whose ranks some of our
friends were missing.

"Our planes, unaided and alone, have destroyed nineteen
enemy ships and damaged sixteen more; in addition they have
assisted in the destruction of ten ships and the damaging of
seven.

"Our pilots have shot down 185 aircraft."

Looking at the ship's officers, Marines and enlisted men,
many of whom were untanned because they had spent two
years almost continuously below decks in the engine-rooms,
he added: "Twice our men have fought off the heaviest air
attacks ever launched against any American ship and, licking
our wounds, we have returned to battle.

"Men of the *Enterprise,* your record has never been even
remotely approached by any ship of this or any other navy.

"In the future no man will be able to serve aboard her
without being inspired by her indomitable spirit and her val-
iant fighting heart.

"Other carriers may come and go, and good ones they are,
but the *Enterprise*—she's the best, she's the champ."

After the citations and awards were presented and the
order "Carry On" was sounded, I saw one man, with tears
in his eyes, walk up the deck and stand looking at a new patch
where a Jap bomb had entered. As I passed him, he awk-
wardly rubbed his shoe over it to see if the patch fit.

Six months later, public recognition was given the Big E.
She was awarded the coveted Presidential Unit Citation—the
highest honor any ship can receive. It was the first such award
given a carrier.

It reads:

The President of the United States takes pleasure in presenting the PRESIDENTIAL UNIT CITATION to the

UNITED STATES SHIP *ENTERPRISE*

for services set forth in the following

CITATION:

For consistently outstanding performance and distinguished achievement during repeated action against enemy Japanese forces in the Pacific War Area, December 7, 1941, to November 15, 1942. Participating in nearly every major carrier engagement in the first year of the war, the ENTERPRISE and her Air Group, exclusive of her far-flung destruction of hostile shore installations throughout the battle area, did sink or damage, on her own, a total of 35 Japanese vessels and shoot down a total of 185 Japanese aircraft. Her aggressive fighting spirit and superb combat efficiency are fitting tribute to the officers and men who so gallantly established her as a solid bulwark in defense of the American Nation.

Gilbert and Marshall Islands Raid	February 1, 1942
Wake Island Raid	February 25, 1942
Marcus Island Raid	March 4, 1942
Battle of Midway	June 4-6, 1942
Occupation of Guadalcanal	August 7-8, 1942
Battle of Stewart Islands	August 24, 1942
Battle of Santa Cruz Islands	October 26, 1942
Battle of Solomon Islands	November 14-15, 1942

For the President,

FRANK KNOX
Secretary of the Navy

The citation was painted on the bulkhead of the ship's hangar deck. Recently I saw a man remove his cap and read it before going into battle.

Not long after, the Big E received this message, which meant almost as much to her men as the citation itself:

To: U.S.S. ENTERPRISE

It is with a deep feeling of pride and gratification that I learn of the Presidential Citation for the *Enterprise*. This eminently deserved award expresses the appreciation of a grateful people for your outstanding accomplishments in this war. Keep fighting, ever mindful of the glorious traditions you have established. My heart is with you always.

HALSEY

Then there was one. Today there are "more than forty" carriers, with more to come, to quote latest official figures, and with these carriers the *Enterprise* is still in the thick of battle. She will be there to the end.

As for what her men think that end will be, I recall John Crommelin's parting in Noumea: "So long, Gene. I'll see you at the end of the war in Yokohama harbor, when we dictate the peace from the deck of the *Enterprise*."

APPENDIX

This story really began in 1933. Under an act approved by Congress on June 16 of that year, President Roosevelt authorized the sum of 238,000,000 dollars for the construction of naval vessels. Time was to prove this one of the wisest investments the United States ever made, but it was indicative of the sorry state of public opinion at the time that the bill was passed by Congress not as a forthright measure of national self-protection, but under the more acceptable illusion that it was "a means of furthering national recovery."

Almost nine years later this sum—a paltry one when compared with the expenditures for armament then going on in Germany and Japan—contributed to a different sort of recovery than we anticipated, recovery from the worst military disaster that ever befell us, the attack on Pearl Harbor. That we recovered at all was a miracle, as this book will show. And the miracle was performed by the heroism, blood and death of many men, against the life of any one of whom the largest sum of money that Congress may ever appropriate is nothing at all.

Following the appropriation, the Navy Department on August 3, 1933, awarded a contract to the Newport News Shipbuilding and Drydock Company for the building of an aircraft carrier. The keel of this vessel was laid on July 16, 1934, and she received the official designation of CV-6. Her name was to be the U.S.S. *Enterprise*.

It was already a famous name in the annals of the Navy. The first ship to paint those letters at her bow was a sloop

(1775-76), captured from the British, which fought success-
fully at Lake Champlain in 1776 under General Benedict
Arnold. The second (1777), an armed schooner, served in
the same war by convoying transports in Chesapeake Bay.

The third (1799-1823), the most famous of the predeces-
sors, was originally a twelve-gun schooner. It won the soubriquet "Lucky little *Enterprise*" by its long, eventful, and bril-
liant career in the war with France, against the Barbary
pirates and in the War of 1812. It was said of her that she
"never met with a reverse, nor a serious mishap; never failed
to capture any antagonist with whom she joined issue in
battle, and when forced to escape from absolutely overwhelming odds, was able to out-distance her pursuers, in one
case, only after a chase of 70 hours." She also had a long list
of famous captains, including Stephen Decatur, Isaac Hull,
and David Porter.

The fourth ship of the name (1831-1844) was a ten-gun
schooner which helped suppress the flourishing West African
slave trade; the fifth (1879-1909) was a steam corvette with
auxiliary sail power which saw duty as a unit of our Euro-
pean squadron until 1891 and was then converted into a cadet
training ship. The naval career of the sixth (1917-1919),
originally a private yacht, was limited to World War I in
which she saw service as a patrol vessel.

The present *Enterprise* has a displacement of 20,000 tons,
a length of 825 feet, and a maximum breadth of 109 feet. She
was built at a cost of approximately nineteen million dollars.
The ship's complement on being commissioned was 82 officers
and 1,447 enlisted men; with an Air Group (originally four
squadrons) aboard, the complement increased to approximately 170 officers and 1,900 enlisted men.

The *Enterprise* was launched on October 3, 1936. She was
christened by Mrs. Claude Swanson, wife of the Secretary of

the Navy, who sent her down the ways with a quotation from *Othello*. As the bottle broke across her bow and the new *Enterprise* took to the water, these words sped her on her way: "May she also say with just pride: 'I have done the State some service.'"

THE U.S.S. ENTERPRISE
A Pictorial Record
Photographs Courtesy of Bureau of Public
Relations, Navy Department.

THE FIRST OFFENSIVE. Crewmen wheel bombs to planes on the Big E's flight deck, just before the attack on the Marshall Islands in February, 1942.

ABOVE: A scout bomber gets ready to take off from the *Enterprise* for the Marshall Islands attack.

BELOW: Off Wotje Island, a Jap plane "came in, sheared off the tail of one of our parked planes, left its wing on the Number 2 gun gallery and slid over the side into the water."

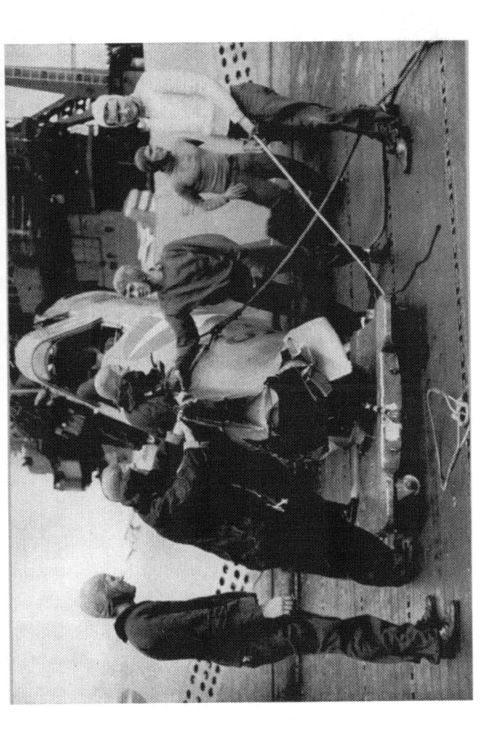

ABOVE: A plane takes off for the attack on Wake Island. The photograph shows the vapor-cloud effect that delayed the Big E pilots.

RIGHT: An *Enterprise* bomber over Wake Island in the February, 1942, raid.

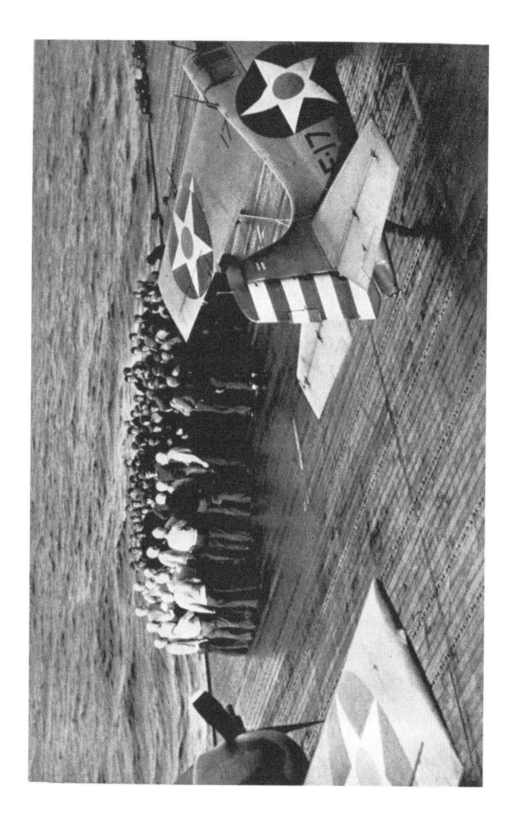

ABOVE: The deck crew of the *Enterprise* get final instructions before the Marcus Island attack in March, 1942.

RIGHT: Fighter planes on the deck of the *Enterprise* are being checked and reloaded after their return from Marcus Island.

ABOVE: The *Hornet* as she appeared from the *Enterprise*, as they sped west for the take-off on the Tokyo raid.

BELOW: The end of the *Lexington*, the first of America's carrier casualties in the first year of the war.

LEFT: This enlargement from an original in 16-mm. film shows dive bombers just before peeling off to smash at Jap warships below, in the Battle of Midway.

BELOW: A Japanese heavy cruiser after being bombed by carrier-based planes at Midway.

ABOVE: Then there were five. The *Yorktown* listing and burning after a Japanese torpedo attack at Midway.

RIGHT: Seen from under the forward overhang of the Big E's flight deck, Lieutenant Turner Caldwell, Jr., and his rear-seatman, Willard Glidewell, take off to attack Jap bases in the Solomons on August 7, 1942. Caldwell later led the group of dive bombers that based on Henderson Field and helped the Marines hold Guadalcanal.

ABOVE: Machinist Eugene Runyan (left, looking at camera) gets a cake with four Rising Suns frosted on top, to celebrate his shooting down four Jap dive bombers in three minutes, in the August fighting off Guadalcanal.

BELOW: The Big E takes it, in the fighting off the Solomons in late August, 1942.

AFTERNOON TAKE-OFF. A Grumman Wildcat takes off from the *Enterprise* to make a combat patrol.

JAP FUNERAL PYRES. Burning oil and black smoke mark the end of Jap planes that tried to crash dive the *Enterprise* in the fighting of late August, 1942. The ship's rail in foreground shows how close they came to succeeding.

DIRECT HIT. The photographer has caught the bomb at the exact moment of exploding on the flight deck of the *Enterprise*, August 24, 1942.

THE BIG E WOUNDED. Crewmen of the *Enterprise* examine the damage done by a Japanese bomb.

ABOVE: Then there were four. Only a few men remain on the forward deck of the *Wasp*, after she was struck by torpedoes on September 15. Later she had to be sunk by our own destroyers.

BELOW: The Big E takes it at Santa Cruz. Japanese planes dive for the *Enterprise* through the cloud of flak.

RUNNING WILD. Shaken loose from its moorings by a near miss, during the Battle of Santa Cruz, a parked plane on the *Enterprise* skitters to the edge of the flight deck.

RUNAWAY SLOWS DOWN. The runaway plane halts just before plunging into the gun gallery.

ABOVE: Crewmen of the *Enterprise* "capture" the runaway plane and haul it away from the gun gallery.

BELOW: Then there was one. Japanese planes attack the *Hornet* at the Battle of Santa Cruz. The dive bomber in the center crashed into the signal bridge of the carrier a moment later.

RIGHT: "Proceed without *Hornet*." These terse words flashed by signboard to a pilot getting ready to take off from the *Enterprise* during the Battle of Santa Cruz tell the news that the Big E is last U. S. carrier left in the South Pacific.

BELOW: The Big E. loses a parked plane as it heels over in a sharp turn as the result of a bomb hit.

ABOVE: The skippers of the *Enterprise:* Captain George D. Murray, Captain Arthur C. Davis, Captain Osborne B. Hardison, and Captain Samuel P. Ginder.

BELOW: A Big E squadron on Guadalcanal. Just as Lieutenant Caldwell and his dive bombers helped to save Guadalcanal in August and September, 1942, this torpedo squadron under Lieutenant Albert P. Coffin used Henderson Field as a base in the November fighting around Guadalcanal, and sank the first Jap battleship sunk by carrier planes.

RIGHT: Big E crewmen unfold the wings of a fighter preparatory to take-off.

BELOW: At sundown, planes of the *Enterprise* are parked on the flight deck.

HONORS. Captain Samuel P. Ginder receives the Presidential Unit Citation from Admiral Chester P. Nimitz aboard the *Enterprise.*

CPSIA information can be obtained
at www.ICGtesting.com
Printed in the USA
BVHW050500200123
656624BV00007B/375